To: Sloan
ACBalbourn 12/14

MW01236113

PAUL SPEAKS TO US TODAY

Our Culture, Our Churches and Our Salvation

by
R.C. Balfour III

ISBN: 978-1-935802-01-3

FATHER
&
SON
PUBLISHING, INC.
4909 North Monroe Street
Tallahassee, Florida 32303-7015
www.fatherson.com
800-741-2712

Dedication

I dedicate this book to the Rev. Chuck Bennett and his wife, Linda. Also to Dick and Nell Jones, and to the elders of Trinity Anglican Church, all of whom have helped me through some difficult times and have always been there for me.

It has been your gracious pleasure, O God, to provide a way out of sin and death for mankind. For in the fullness of time You sent your Son born of a woman to redeem and save us. . . Pauline thought.

Acknowledgments

I owe a great debt of gratitude to two clergymen who were kind enough to read and critique my manuscript: the Rev. Chuck Bennett and the Rev. Jim Hobby. As always, I thank my wife, Virginia, who has been an invaluable assistant in identifying scripture, offering ideas, and proofreading. Anne King, who was already involved in a busy schedule, again did the final proofreading, correcting grammar and punctuation. Robert L. Crawford converted my manuscript to book form. Thanks to the Rev. Bob Dixon for the text illustrations. And more than ever, I am thankful for the guidance of the Holy Spirit, without whom I never could have completed the manuscript.

.

Other Books by R. C. Balfour III

In Search of the Aucilla

Fishing for the Abundant Life

He Turned the World Upside Down

Introduction
A Mighty Fortress Against Revisionism

The words of St. Paul are as alive today as they were two thousand years ago. One of his constant themes is the warning against *another gospel*. In Paul's own words, "...there are some who trouble you and want to pervert the gospel of Christ. But even if we, or an angel from heaven, should preach to you a gospel contrary to that which we preached to you, let him be accursed!"[1] The Judaizers[2] were following behind Paul and in every instance proposing a different gospel to the fledgling congregations. This made Paul's work even harder, but fortunately for us today, his clear defense of the Gospel, given to him by Christ, can be used against those who propose a Gospel created by mankind to fit the culture and mores of today's society.

Paul's letters plainly reveal *God's plan* for mankind's

---

[1] Gal. 1:7b,8 RSV.
[2] Jews who believed in Jesus, but also demanded that the Gentile converts be circumcised and follow the whole law of Moses.

redemption and salvation. They are filled with words of pure truth about God and mankind. Many of his statements bring tears of appreciation and esteem to those who are seeking God. It is with this in mind that I have sought to write a story of Paul's life based closely upon Acts, but with just a ring of adventure and suspense. In some chapters I have also sought to enlarge upon Paul's faith and theology.

In our world today there are many voices who attempt to preach the Gospel, some true and some false. By using Paul's words as a test or a template we can ascertain the true or false nature of what we hear or read; we can hold fast to *God's plan* of salvation.

I have no argument with those who contend that Paul lived in a patriarchal society and that he was influenced by Hebrew scripture. I will cover these subjects in the following chapters, but on the whole Paul was far ahead of his time and reached eons ahead of the prevailing values and traditions of his age.

But why another book about Paul? In my case it was an imperative. Paul was instrumental in converting me to the basic Gospel—to faith in Jesus Christ. He rescued me from believing that Christianity was just a set of rules or laws (which I was never able to completely follow). He showed me what faith in Christ alone could accomplish. I developed a love for Jesus which changed my heart and gave me a burning desire to please and follow him.

Also, I found some of the most compelling books on Paul to be a little esoteric or scholarly. I have tried to write a clear, straight forward and accurate version that is, I hope, easy to understand. My readers will be the best judge of how well I succeeded. To avoid any confusion, I must warn readers that, although the book is not a novel, I have used a small amount of "poetic license" or perhaps "spiritual imagination" when neither Acts nor the letters fill in the complete story.

Also, I must make it clear that this book is not in any way hostile to the Jews or Judaism. Paul himself believed that the Jews would be brought in at a time of God's choosing. In Romans he writes, "They are the Israelites, and to them belong the sonship, the glory, the covenants, the giving of the law, the worship, and the promises; to them belong the patriarchs, and of their race, according to the flesh, is the Christ..."[3] Paul never gave up on his own people.

I have not capitalized the personal pronouns referring to the Father, the Son, and the Holy Spirit (except in a handful of instances necessary to distinguish identity). This follows the practice found in the RSV, NRSV, NIV, and King James translations of the Holy Bible. Neither have I capitalized the word "sabbath" following the practice in the RSV, NRSV and King James translations. On the other hand I have capitalized the word "Gospel" when referring to the Gospel of Jesus Christ (except in Bible quotations). I did this since in some modern uses "gospel" refers to the real truth about other subjects, for example "That's the gospel" or "that's the gospel truth."

Finally, for clarity, we placed Bible quotations in italics when someone other than Paul was speaking or writing.

R.C. Balfour III

---

[3] Rom.9:4-5a RSV.

Prologue

Seldom in the history of civilization has one man had such an enormous effect upon the world. In his role as an evangelist and its effect upon Asia, Asia Minor and Europe, Paul stands alone. Likewise, in his role as a theologian and its effect upon all the ages and countries of the world, Paul is without peer among mortals.

If his evangelism converted thousands, his letters have converted many more. They have a quality of intellect, faith, history and poignancy hardly ever found in one man's writing. Essentially, they were letters in response to questions posed by the early church. That gives them the ring of authenticity, lacking in works which deal mainly in theory or symbols.

In his unrelenting drive to spread the Gospel, Paul was a man torn between the love of his own people, the Jews, and his commission to preach to the Gentiles. At every turn the unbelieving Jews sought to still his voice—to kill him. Even in this atmosphere, Paul continued trying to persuade them that Jesus was the Messiah. He never gave up on this goal, which contributed to his constant tribulations.

Paul's final evangelistic goal was to preach the Gospel in Spain. He wrote to the Romans, "I hope to see you in passing as I go to Spain, and to be sped on my journey there by you, once I have enjoyed your company for a little."[4] He then explained that he had to go to Jerusalem to deliver the collection from the new churches in Greece, Asia and Asia Minor to the poor among the saints. Then he would set out for Spain by way of Rome.

It was that last trip to Jerusalem which resulted in Paul's direct confrontation with the Sanhedrin, the highest Jewish deliberative body. Acts does not tell us whether he ever reached Spain. This tantalizing question is still open for scholars to theorize and speculate on—a ripe field for mystery, investigation, and imagination.

---

[4] Rom. 15:24 RSV.

1

The Making Of A Vicious Persecutor

The crowd had gathered and was growing. At first, single accusations were shouted in fierce anger.

"He has preached against our law and ancestors!"

"He brought Greeks into the temple!"

"He should die. Away with him!"

Soon voices blended into an uproar as the mob surged into the temple looking for Paul. They dragged him out and began kicking him and beating him with their fists.

While they were trying to kill him, word of the disturbance came to the Roman tribune. Immediately he assembled some soldiers and quickly ran to the temple. When the mob saw him, they stopped beating Paul and drew back. The tribune ordered Paul to be bound with chains and then inquired what Paul had done. Some shouted one thing and some another. The clamor of voices grew so loud the tribune ordered that Paul be brought into the barracks. Even then, the crowd pressed in so close that Paul had to be carried by the soldiers.

As Paul was about to enter the barracks, he appealed to the tribune in Greek, asking permission to address the crowd. Surprised that Paul spoke Greek, the tribune, realizing that he was not a suspected Egyptian assassin, allowed him to speak. Paul, standing on the steps, motioned for silence and addressed the crowd in Hebrew .

He began, "I am a Jew, born in Tarsus in Cilicia, but brought up in this city at the feet of Gamaliel, educated strictly according to our ancestral law, being zealous for God, just as all of you are today...."[1] And so started the final tribulations Paul faced which would carry him all the way to Rome.

Saul [2] was born of Hebrew parents in the great Roman city of Tarsus, located on the northeast corner of the Mediterranean. The Taurus Mountains guarded its north while the Cnidus River and a great lake made it a natural inland port only ten miles from the sea. Many years before, Mark Antony met the

---

[1] Acts 22:3 NRSV.

[2] Paul's Hebrew name used through Acts Chapter 12, probably named after the first king of Israel.

captivating Cleopatra here and gave Roman citizenship to all its citizens.[3]

The city possessed other great advantages. It not only enjoyed significant maritime trade, but also was located on an important east-west trade route. A great university sprang up in Tarsus, rivaling the intellectual climate of Athens and even Alexandria. Stoic philosophers flourished there, and the city greatly valued its civic and democratic ideals. Such was the culture of the city where Saul grew up.

His parents, however, were strict Pharisees, so the first thing Saul heard each morning was the Shema:

> *"Hear, O Israel: The Lord our God is one Lord, and you shall love the Lord your God with all your heart, and with all your soul, and with all your might."*

His Jewish father was further instructed:

> *"...you shall teach them (these words) diligently to your children, and shall talk of them when you sit in your house, and when you walk by the way and when you lie down and when you rise."*[4]

During morning prayer, Saul was also required to wear phylacteries, small leather cases in which quotations from the Hebrew scripture were stored.

Saul had a brilliant and inquiring mind. As he grew older, he was exposed to the Greek culture of Tarsus and very likely attended some classes at Tarsus University. He thereby acquired a firm grasp of Greek philosophy and language. Hellenist (Greek) influence prompted his parents' decision to send the

---

[3] M.S. Miller and J.L. Miller, *Harper's Bible Dictionary,* Harper and Row, *New York, N.Y, 1952, 1954,1955, ,1956, 1958, 1959, 1961, p 727.*
[4] Both quotations are from Deut. 6:4-7 RSV (my parenthesis).

young man to Jerusalem to study under the renowned Rabbi Gamaliel.

Saul was not especially handsome, but something (perhaps his piercing eyes and sincere facial expressions) drew people to him, especially when he spoke. He also had a commanding presence, suggesting a young man with a full head of black hair and a black beard. The tremendous endurance and harsh punishments later encountered on his long journeys indicate that he possessed a strong muscular body[5].

Under the instruction of Gamaliel, Saul quickly became zealous of his Jewish ancestry and faith. With his great intellect, he surpassed other students especially in his grasp of Jewish scripture, religious customs, and the law.

Jerusalem, about 37 AD was in turmoil. Although long ruled by the Romans, some local autonomy was allowed, culminating in the Sanhedrin, a Jewish deliberative body made up of Jewish religious leaders including Pharisees, Sadducees and even a few Zealots. Its powers were strictly limited, but were in keeping with the Roman practice of allowing limited local rule. It was generally presided over by the High Priest.

The strict practitioners of Jewish customs and the law were very nervous about a sect calling themselves The Way. These were disciples of Jesus Christ. Their numbers had increased to an alarming extent and the Sanhedrin was fearful of their growing influence. The Jews needed a charismatic leader firmly

---

[5] The largely comical description of an early century writer (in the opinion of this author) does not fit the actions and accomplishments of Paul.

established in Jewish law and faith to combat the growing movement.

When young Saul was brought to their attention, they were fascinated by his aggressive attitude toward the defense of their heritage and faith. In him they found the youth, energy, conviction and temperament needed in an effective prosecutor. The chief priests quickly empowered him with the office and papers necessary to prosecute The Way. He was even elevated to a position in the Sanhedrin in order that his testimony and vote might be counted against followers of Jesus. For Saul, this was a great opportunity to show his ability, determination, and absolute loyalty to his Jewish heritage. It would promote him far above other Jews his same age and advance him further in the Jewish hierarchy. [6]

Saul, in his fanatic Jewish conviction, became like a roaring beast attacking followers of The Way with imprisonment and murder. Saul presided over the killing of Stephen, one of seven elected by the apostles to help in the daily distribution of food. Stephen was full of the Holy Spirit and did many signs and wonders among the people. But there was a group of Jews from Alexandria and Asia who opposed Stephen and argued with him openly. This group stirred up people to stand before the council [7] and accuse him of perverting the Jewish faith and blaspheming Moses and God.

In his own defense, Stephen guided by the Holy Spirit, made

---

[6] Acts 26:9,10. The fact that Saul possessed a vote indicates that he was probably a member of the Sanhedrin.

[7] Another name for the Sanhedrin.

a brilliant speech before the council, tracing the whole history of the Jews from Abraham to Jesus and accusing the Jews of killing the prophets and the Righteous One, the Messiah Jesus. Hearing his eloquent history and sharp accusations, the council became enraged and embittered. They turned Stephen over to the prosecutor to be put to death.

With Saul in charge, the mob dragged Stephen out of the city and began stoning him. Stone after stone racked his body until he was covered with blood. His breathing became shallow and he fell to his knees, praying, "Lord Jesus, receive my spirit." And as he was dying, he shouted out with his last breath, "Lord, do not hold this sin against them."

"That day a severe persecution began against the church in Jerusalem, and all except the apostles were scattered throughout the countryside of Judea and Samaria....But Saul was ravaging the church by entering house after house; dragging off both men and women, he committed them to prison."[8]

After his merciless attacks and murder against the disciples of Jesus in Jerusalem, Saul went to the High Priest and asked for letters to the synagogues in Damascus. He was intent upon finding any belonging to The Way in that city so that he might bring them bound to Jerusalem for imprisonment and punishment

---

[8] Acts 8:1,3 NRSV.

2

The Light Reflected
Around The World

Saul's small caravan had completed most of the 150 miles from Jerusalem to Damascus over a rocky and sandy road. Just coming into view was the sparkling green oasis of Damascus fed by a river which divided into many streams, watering the entire city. The oasis contained orchards and fertile fields which produced an abundance of fruits and grains. An entire week had been consumed by the trip, and sighting the beautiful oasis in the midst of the arid land lifted the spirits of the men. The caravan was drawing nearer Damascus when a light brighter than the sun shone around them. The light was overwhelming and bore down hard, driving the men to the ground.

Saul rolled over, opened his eyes and gazed directly into the light. He heard a voice in Hebrew saying, "Saul, Saul, why do you persecute me?"

Saul asked, "Who are you, Lord?"

"I am Jesus, whom you are persecuting. I have appeared to appoint you as my witness to the Gentiles and the people of Israel. I am sending you to them, that they might turn from darkness to light—from the power of Satan to God. I will be with you so that Jews and Gentiles may receive forgiveness of sins and be sanctified by faith in me. Get up and go into the city, and you will be told what to do."[1]

Saul, thoroughly shaken, struggled to his feet, and though his eyes were open, they had no features. They appeared as one born blind; he could see nothing. The strong, relentless prosecutor was utterly bewildered and helpless. Finally one of the men accompanying him took his arm and led him stumbling into the city. For three days he was blind and ate or drank nothing.

There was a certain dedicated disciple living in Damascus named Ananias. The Lord appeared to him in a vision and instructed him to go to the house of Judas on Straight Street. There he would find a helpless man named Saul. The Lord further instructed Ananias to go and lay hands on Saul so that he might recover his sight. At first Ananias protested for he was aware of Saul's reputation. But the Lord continued, "Go, for *I have chosen him as an instrument* to bring my name before the

---

[1] Based on Acts 26:13-18.

Gentiles and the people of Israel. I will show him how much he must suffer for the sake of my name."

So Ananias went, entered the house and found Saul praying. "He laid his hands on Saul and said, 'Brother Saul, the Lord Jesus, who appeared to you on your way here, has sent me so that you may regain your sight and be filled with the Holy Spirit' And immediately something like scales fell from his eyes and his sight was restored."[2] As the Spirit fell upon Saul, his tangled thoughts and whirling mind began to slow down. All at once a strange peace came upon him. At the same time he felt an irrepressible passion to tell the world that Jesus was alive—that he was the Messiah. He got up and was baptized, and after eating some food, regained his strength.

What followed is one of the most amazing stories ever told. The conversion of Saul is the greatest conversion in history, and his life became one of adventure, hardship and a dedication surpassing that of his former life. Saul had been carefully trained in Judaism by his parents since birth, and every day had been a further advance in that faith. He had studied hard and meticulously under one of the greatest of all rabbis, Gamaliel, and his dedication to Judaism had been recognized by the foremost leaders and scholars in Jerusalem. Consequently, the change which occurred on the Damascus road was truly miraculous. This conclusion is further enforced by the fact that the change was not temporary but lasted his whole lifetime and was challenged and tested consistently by the most brutal circumstances.

Saul stayed with the believers in Damascus for a short time

---

[2] Act 9:17, 18a NRSV.

and then went into the nearby desert of Arabia.[3] In the desert Saul had visions of Jesus, who also spoke directly to him. One night with the stars and moon shining so bright that the desert was illuminated, Saul, half awake and half asleep, saw Jesus at table with the twelve apostles. He saw Jesus take a loaf of bread, and when he had given thanks, he broke it and said, "This is my body that is for you. Do this in remembrance of me." In the same way he took the cup also, after supper, saying, "This cup is the new covenant in my blood. Do this, as often as you drink it in remembrance of me. For as often as you eat this bread and drink this cup you proclaim the Lord's death until he comes.."[4]

Months later, while asleep on the desert floor, another vision came to Saul. This one was so real and intense, it made Saul break out in a cold sweat and shake uncontrollably. A man was being stripped of his clothes and laid upon a crude wooden cross. Iron spikes were driven into his hands and his feet, the blood dripping upon the ground. His only words were, "Father, forgive them, for they know not what they do." He was then hoisted into the air between two criminals. And even though the agony was displayed upon the man's face, he never cried out. Just then, Saul recognized the face. It was the face of the man who had taken the last supper with the apostles. It was the Lord Jesus.

One day, after his noon meal, Saul halfway drifted off to sleep. This time he distinctly saw an empty tomb, with grave clothes neatly wrapped up and placed at the head and the foot of

---

[3] This passage is based on Gal.1:16b and 17 which states, "I did not confer with flesh and blood, nor did I go up to Jerusalem to those who were apostles before me, but I went into Arabia." RSV.

[4] 1 Cor. 11:24-26 NRSV. This is probably the first written account of the Eucharist or Communion, the letters having been written before the Gospels.

the rock shelf. The scene shifted and he saw Jesus talking to a crowd of over 500 of his disciples. His raiments were very bright, and his voice was like the sound of many running waters.

In these times of isolation, prayer, and contemplation, Jesus spoke to Saul, giving him more details of the new covenant and the commission of carrying the Gospel to the Gentile nations and to the world. This became a time of prayer, study and complete re-interpretation of scripture. It was his preparation for the enormous task of taking the Gospel to the Gentile nations while always trying to persuade his own people of the Gospel truth. His conversion became the single driving force in his life as he wrote in Philippians, "…I regard everything as loss because of the surpassing value of knowing Christ Jesus my Lord. For his sake I have suffered the loss of all things, and I regard them as rubbish, in order that I may gain Christ and be found in him…"[5]

Saul returned to Damascus and immediately began proclaiming Jesus to be the Son of God. His enthusiastic preaching amazed not only those of The Way, but also confounded the Jews who did not believe. They lost no time in planning to kill him. But what they did not realize was that God, through Christ, had recruited their best "player" to take the lead in manifesting Christ to the world. It is certain that Christ had his eyes on Saul long before the chief priests employed him.

Watchmen were posted at every city gate of Damascus to keep Saul from escaping, but at night the brothers[6] let him down in a basket through a hole in the wall. So, narrowly escaping the Jews of Damascus, he went to Jerusalem, speaking boldly in the

---

[5] Philippians 3: 8, 9a NRSV.
[6] "Brothers" was a term commonly used to denote fellow Christians, not in any sense blood kin.

name of Jesus. He was introduced to some of the apostles, but his rhetoric so angered the Hellenist Jews of the Synagogue that they tried to kill him. For his own safety, the believers sent him off to Tarsus.

The problem in Saul's day was not a lack of religions. The Mediterranean world was awash in religions. There were pagan Greek gods and goddesses amplified by those of Rome. There were Greek mystery cults. Almost every large city had a special deity such as the "great Artemis of the Ephesians." In addition, schools of Greek philosophy abounded—Stoic and Epicurean, advocates of Plato and Socrates, and others. Such philosophies bordered on religions. And, of course, the most comprehensive and complete of all was Judaism, led and variously blessed by God (Yahweh) himself and resting on the Pentateuch—the first five books of the Old Testament with the delineation of moral and ceremonial laws.

Even in Israel there were different schools of thought. Pharisees were strict practitioners of the law; Sadducees were worldly and friendlier with the Romans. Herodians supported the Roman government, while Zealots were fully convinced that Yahweh was leading them to overthrow Roman rule and establish a political kingdom of God. Essenes were a monastic group, living almost apart from the others with their own interpretation of scripture.

What chance did the small band of The Way have in such different cultures? From a worldly point of view—none. But The Way possessed vital elements the others lacked. The God of the universe had established their roots and given them the law and the prophets. Furthermore, he had sent his Son to redeem them and become the first of those who would be raised from the dead and given an incorruptible body. Essentially, he had given them an eschatology—a confidence in their own individual salvation stretching into an unlimited future. This faith was made sure and fortified by the coming of the Holy Spirit, enabling them to work miracles of healing and exorcism. And Jesus had picked Saul, one of the most gifted intellectuals of his time and a man of unbelievable fortitude and tenacity, to carry the Gospel to the world.

Saul was a Pharisee, but with the astounding Damascus road conversion and further contacts with the Lord Jesus, he was being molded into the Apostle to the Gentiles. And as strange as it seemed to the unbelieving Jews, this would fulfill the promise of God to Abraham that his seed would bless every nation.

During his years in the Arabian Desert, Saul, with help of the Lord, finished formulating his faith. That faith faced hostile cultures, fierce opposition from his own people, and persecution. But the light which shone around Saul was never extinguished. It continues today in hostile cultures and faces opposition which would like to smother it forever, but Saul's faith is just as valid and the light just as brilliant as it was 2000 years ago. In a world being torn apart by self-indulgence, greed, immorality, and bitter antagonism, that same light is the only hope of mankind.

3

The Major Hurdle For Paul's Theology

Deuteronomy 21:23b states, "…for anyone hung on a tree is under God's curse." In that context the statement applies to the vilest criminal, but the Jews of Saul's day, especially the Pharisees, applied it to Jesus. So when Jesus' disciples claimed that he was the Messiah, the Jews thought it was blasphemy.

This very assumption was partly responsible for Saul's energetic persecution of the people of The Way. When Jesus appeared to Saul on the road to Damascus, it was immediately evident that the crucified one was alive, had risen from the grave. Saul had both seen and heard the living Lord in the brilliant light which shone about him. Jesus was indeed the

Anointed One, spoken of by Moses, David, and the prophets.

The initial shock of this event must have been overwhelming for Saul as he groped his way into the city. But after Ananias laid hands upon him, and after he had received the Holy Spirit and had been baptized, his head became clearer.

However, it was in the three years Saul spent in the Arabian Desert, having visions and talking to Jesus that his theology of the cross became crystal clear. He would later write about the cross and its meaning for all mankind, making it the central theme of his theology. There are many in our times who still don't understand its meaning and some who want to eliminate it from the Gospel.

"O the depth of the riches and wisdom and knowledge of God! How unsearchable are his judgments and how inscrutable his ways!"[1] We are quite often mistaken when we believe God will act a certain way to establish his truth, his way, and his kingdom. In sending his Son to die on the cross, our human way of thinking tends to reject such an approach. First of all, we must understand that the crucifixion and resurrection were acts of God in which he was fully present. In Colossians Paul declared, "For in him (Jesus) all the fullness of God was pleased to dwell."

In contrast to the almost complete power of the Roman Empire and the radical ancestral tradition of the Jews, God chose the cruelest and most feared instrument of the time—the

---

[1] Rom. 11:33 NRSV.

16

cross—to introduce his gift of salvation to the world. *God's love met human arrogance, brute force, hate, injustice and pride at the cross and defeated them all.*

Paul's whole theology was turned upside down when he met the risen and exalted Christ on the read to Damascus. The crucified one was indeed God's exalted one; the cross became the beginning of the transformational process for all baptized believers. High position, power, wealth and most human values faced a meltdown under the brightness of God's grace. God revealed himself in the crucifixion and resurrection of Jesus Christ, who became the central figure in the salvation process. This is what led Paul to write, "For I decided to know nothing among you except Jesus Christ and him crucified,"[2] an expression which still mystifies some Christians.

Paul in 1st Corinthians wrote, "…but we proclaim Christ crucified, a stumbling block to the Jews and foolishness to Gentiles, but *to those who are the called*, both Jews and Greeks, Christ the power of God and the wisdom of God. For God's foolishness is wiser than human wisdom, and God's weakness is stronger than human strength…But God chose what is foolish in the world to shame the wise; God chose what is weak in the world to shame the strong;…He is the source of your life in Christ Jesus, who became for us wisdom from God and righteousness and sanctification and redemption."[3]

"The saying is sure and worthy of full acceptance, that Christ Jesus came into the world to save sinners."[4] On the cross God in Christ took upon himself all the sins of humanity including

---

[2] 1st Cor. 2:2 RSV.
[3] 1st Cor. 1:23-30 NRSV.
[4] 1st Tim. 1:15 RSV.

the ones of pride, jealously, and hate directed against him. When Christ died as the likeness of the old Adam, these transgressions and sins died also. God, in his love for his creation and creatures, abolished our sins, *offering* to all who would accept his way a full pardon and a new life. However, the cross without the resurrection would not be complete. Christ was resurrected on the third day, defeating mankind's oldest enemy, death, and triumphing over Satan and all worldly powers including the Roman Empire and the Jewish Sanhedrin.

God used love instead of force to redeem mankind—a totally unexpected turn of events. Without using his immense power to destroy, God used his power of love to *offer* redemption and salvation to all believers, obliterating previously committed sins. Paul characterizes this as proof of God's righteousness. Salvation became a matter of changing the heart more than the mind.

Paul wrote to the Colossians, "…when you were buried with him (Jesus) in baptism, you were also raised with him through faith in the power of God, who raised him from the dead…He forgave us all our trespasses, erasing the record that stood against us with its legal demands. He set this aside, nailing it to the cross. He disarmed the rulers and authorities and made a public example of them, triumphing over them in it. "[5]

Paul stated that the Gospel had been delivered to him directly by the Lord,[6] but he was diligent in checking it out later with the apostles in Jerusalem. He warned his churches about accepting *another gospel*. The crucifixion and resurrection of Jesus Christ

---

[5] Col. 2:12,13b-15 NRSV.(my parenthesis)
[6] Based on Gal. 1:11,12.

18

was an historical fact that could be confirmed by eye witnesses. Even more important, it was a transcendent act of God *fulfilling God's plan and purpose in redeeming mankind.* It was an ever to be blessed act of grace and could be accomplished only by the initiative of the Creator.

Paul's warning should be taken to heart by many today, who deny that God still acts in his world—that he brings about miracles of deliverance and healing. Some also deny that the Gospel as preached by Paul is as valid now as it was 2000 years ago. Some Christians even try to remove the cross from the Gospel. *Let all mankind seriously consider accepting God's offer of salvation. And let Christians be warned about those, cleric or not, who would attempt to proclaim "another gospel."*

4

The Fire Begins
To Spread

About the time of the persecution which resulted in Stephen's death, many of the believing Jews fled Jerusalem. Some made their way to Antioch of Syria which was located about 300 miles north of Jerusalem. Antioch was one of the largest and more prominent cities of the Roman Empire. The Jewish believers in Antioch accepted Gentiles and it was here that the people of The Way were first called Christians.

The news of the Gentiles' conversion reached the church in Jerusalem and they sent Barnabas (whose name means Son of Encouragement) to Antioch to discern what was happening and to help the church there. Barnabas brings to mind a large man over six feet tall with a premature white flowing beard. Being filled with the Holy Spirit, his face reflected the gentleness and kindness of his personality. His appearance was made even more impressive by his habit of wearing white robes. When he arrived he found the church alive and active in the Spirit, and he encouraged them to remain faithful to the Lord. Barnabas stayed in Antioch for several months. His inspiration and devotion greatly added to the fellowship of the church, and many people were brought to the Lord.

When the church gathered for prayer and praise, Barnabas could actually feel the powerful presence of the Spirit. That is when he began to envision the great potential this Spirit-filled fellowship possessed for the Lord. Privately, he prayed daily for guidance and discernment. It was in one of these prayer times that Saul, whom he had met in Jerusalem, came to mind. Saul's sincerity and enthusiastic preaching had led Barnabas to introduce him to Peter and James, the brother of Jesus. He was also one of the believers who sent Saul off to Tarsus out of the reach of the unbelieving Jews.

Barnabas could not get Saul out of his mind, so he made his way around the eastern shore of the Mediterranean to Tarsus. There he found Saul in the company of other artisans weaving goats' hair into cloth for tent making. Saul was so intent upon his work that he failed to see Barnabas approaching until the big man slapped him on the back. Turning in surprise Saul immediately recognized the one who had introduced him to Peter and James more than ten years earlier. The two disciples hugged each other and exchanged warm greetings. Then Barnabas spoke, " Brother Saul, I have found you in hopes of persuading you to come to Antioch—to join a remarkable group of believers who are experiencing the fire of the Holy Spirit."

The two men went out to find some lunch while Barnabas further described the miraculous fellowship in Antioch. Neither Acts nor the letters are very clear about Saul's activities during the years before Barnabas's visit.[1] Realizing the greater potential of fulfilling his commission, he quickly accepted Barnabas' offer. After settling his accounts and bidding his aging parents farewell, he packed a few belongings and joined Barnabas for the trip back to Antioch.

Worshiping daily in the company of Spirit-filled Christians, Saul began to experience the wonderful fellowship of believers. As they all joined in songs and hymns of praise, Saul also felt the amazing glow of the Spirit.

About this time a prophet named Agabus came down from Jerusalem. He stood up before the church and predicted that a famine would take place over all the world. The disciples decided that each one would give according to his own means to the poor brothers in Jerusalem. Saul and Barnabas were sent there with the relief funds. Saul would later receive an additional collection from the new churches to carry to Jerusalem. Its implications would have ominous consequences for his future.

Saul and Barnabas returned to Antioch, bringing John Mark with them. The church of Jewish and Gentile believers continued to flourish under the guidance of the Holy Spirit, who

---

[1] In Galatian's Chapter 1, Paul simply writes that he went into the regions of Syria and Cilicia (Tarsus), and that word spread to Jerusalem about his preaching Jesus as Messiah. He might have preached secretly in Tarsus in order to protect his parents from the Jews.

directed them to set aside Saul and Barnabas for missionary work. They recruited John Mark, departed for the port of Seleucia and set sail for Cyprus. The first of the extraordinary missionary journeys had begun.

Since the church of today seems to have such a hard time with the doctrine of the Holy Spirit, it is desirable to carefully examine the scripture's understanding as well as Paul's[2] view. In the very beginning, the King James Bible tells us that God created the heaven and the earth (the entire universe). The earth was dark and without form until the Spirit of God moved upon it. The Spirit could be conceived of as the power or energy of God.

Long before Paul, in the salvation history of the Jews, the Holy Spirit of God came upon important figures who were called upon to accomplish difficult tasks. Later, the Spirit fell upon the prophets of Israel, who were led to speak the word of God. It was not until the prophet Joel that any thought was given to the Spirit falling upon common people. Joel, speaking the words of the Lord, proclaimed, "I will pour out My Spirit on all mankind; and your sons and daughters will prophesy…Even on the male and female servants I will pour out My Spirit in those days."[3]

---

[2] Saul was the Jewish name; Paul, the Roman name which Acts uses, starting in Chapter 13.

[3] Joel 2:28a, 29 NASB.

John the Baptist said of Jesus, "I have baptized with water; but he will baptize you with the Holy Spirit."[4] After the Spirit came upon the apostles at Pentecost, they were enabled to do mighty acts in the name of Jesus by the power of the Spirit. Later, when Peter was led to visit the home of Cornelius, a Gentile, and spoke the Gospel to his household, the Spirit came upon all who heard the message of salvation. The scripture says that they spoke in tongues and extolled God. This event went a long way toward convincing the apostles that the message of salvation was meant also for the Gentiles—that they too had received the Holy Spirit.

It is certain that the church at Antioch was powerfully filled with the Holy Spirit. That is why it became a dynamo of prophesy, discernment, witness and evangelism. The fact that it was composed of Jews and Gentiles, black and white, rich and poor[5] seemed to draw God's intense blessing and presence of the Spirit. It was only in such an exceptional fellowship that the Holy Spirit inspired and directed the first missionary journey. Antioch also remained the spiritual base for the journeys which followed.

The Spirit came upon Paul shortly after his Damascus Road encounter with Jesus. It occurred when Ananias laid hands upon him. The Spirit accompanied and blessed Paul on his journeys. He wrote to the Thessalonians, "…our gospel did not come to you in word only, but also in power and in the Holy Spirit and with full conviction…. You also became imitators of us and of

---

[4] Mark 1:8 NRSV.

[5] Acts 13:1.

the Lord, having received the word in much tribulation with the joy of the Holy Spirit."[6]

Receiving the Holy Spirit was the experience of all who heard the Gospel and believed. Paul considered this experience essential to the transition to Christ and ultimate salvation. "But it is God who establishes us with you in Christ and has anointed us, by putting his seal on us and giving us his Spirit in our hearts as a first installment…,"[7] he wrote to the Corinthians. And in comparison to the law, Paul wrote, "… our competence is from God, who has made us competent to be ministers of a new covenant, not of letter but of spirit, for the letter kills, but the Spirit gives life."[8]

In 2nd Corinthians Paul wrote, "For we know that if this earthly tent we live in is destroyed, we have a building from God, a house not made with hands, eternal in the heavens….He who has prepared us for this very thing is God, who has given us the Spirit as a guarantee." Second only to the resurrection of Christ, the Holy Spirit inspired, led, and enabled the early Christians to persevere. This is in sharp contrast to today's view (outside of Pentecostal and charismatic churches), which sometimes treats the Holy Spirit as a subject of intellectual analysis or theological speculation.

Paul set forth the Spirit as the determinant factor, not only in the new life on earth, but also in the resurrection of the dead.

"For those who live according to the flesh set their minds on the things of the flesh, but those who live according to the Spirit

---

[6] 1 Thess. 1:5a, 6 NASB.

[7] 2 Cor. 1: 21, 22 NRSV.

[8] 2 Cor. 3: 5b, 6 NRSV.

set their minds on the things of the Spirit. To set the mind on the flesh is death, but to set the mind on the Spirit is life and peace…. Anyone who does not have the Spirit of Christ does not belong to him….If the Spirit of him who raised Jesus from the dead dwells in you, he who raised Christ from the dead will give life to your mortal bodies also through his Spirit that dwells in you."[9]

In many churches today, it is the sacrament—baptism, followed by the laying on of hands, which petitions the Spirit to fall upon the initiate. In too many cases, however, this experience is ill-defined or nebulous and its teaching anything but clear. In Paul's day, having experienced the reception of the Holy Spirit was the absolute sign of belonging to Christ and becoming one of God's sons or daughters (Romans 8).

There were a number of certain signs of having received the Spirit. They ranged from the spectacular—prophecy,[10] tongues, words of knowledge, and healings, through joyful illumination to moral reformation. These gifts of the Spirit were called charisms, and they were dealt out to different individuals as the Spirit saw fit. Paul wrote, "All these are activated by one and the same Spirit, who allots to each one individually just as the Spirit chooses."[11] In each case a very noticeable and substantial change took place, with the person manifesting the fruit of the Spirit. Paul described the fruit as love, joy, peace, patience,

---

[9] Rom. 8: 5, 6, 9b, 11 NRSV.

[10] Prophecy was not primarily predicting the future, but consisted of speaking the word of God in exhortation, encouragement, or truth spoken in love.

[11] 1 Cor. 12:11 NRSV.

kindness, goodness, faithfulness, gentleness, and self-control.[12] Just think of the difference it would make today—if all Christians manifested these qualities constantly.

Paul was also wise enough to advise that the spectacular gifts be validated and tested by the congregation, so that ecstatic utterances, for instance, when used in worship were always interpreted and done in good order. Two or three were advised to be spoken, no more. Likewise he advised that only two or three prophets speak, letting the congregation weigh what was being said. "God is a God not of disorder but of peace....So my friends, be eager to prophesy, and do not forbid speaking in tongues; but all things should be done decently and in order."[13] After being filled with the Spirit, Paul had a completely changed life. He wrote the Corinthians, "My speech and my proclamation were not with plausible words of wisdom, but with a demonstration of the Spirit and of power so that your faith might rest not on human wisdom but on the power of God."[14] According to scripture, he did many deeds of power including healings as well as rebukes. By the Spirit, he persevered in the most adverse circumstances and accomplished the mission given to him by Christ. *God grant that we recognize and listen to the Holy Spirit today in our worship and in our efforts to carry out the mission given to us by Christ. Amen.*

---

[12] Gal. 5:22, 23a RSV.

[13] 1 Cor. 14:33a, 39, 40 NRSV.

[14] 1 Cor. 2:4,5 NRSV.

5

The Missionary Effort
Bears Fruit

The first missionary journey was well under way when the evangelists reached Lystra, a city in Asia Minor. Paul was preaching there when he observed a man crippled from birth. Gazing intently into the man's face, Paul discerned there the faith to be healed. So in a loud voice Paul commanded, "stand up on your feet." The man immediately sprang to his feet and began walking.

The crowd standing by interpreted this miraculous event in terms of their own religion. One shouted, "The gods have come down to us."

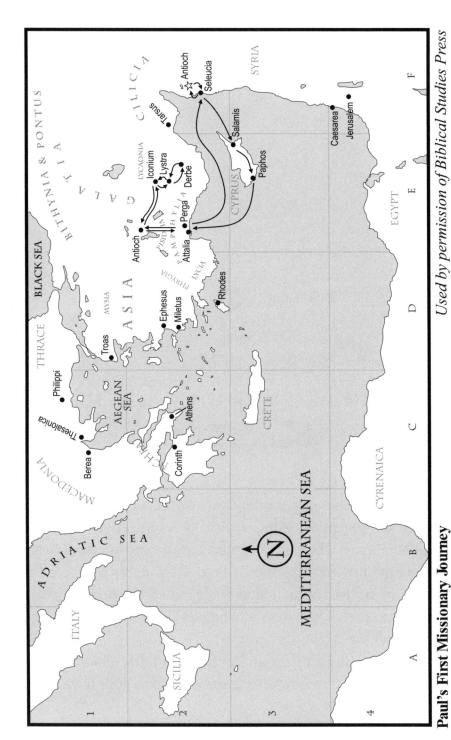

Paul's First Missionary Journey

Used by permission of Biblical Studies Press

Another said, "The one who speaks is Hermes, and the great one (Barnabas) is Zeus!"

The crowd rushed together to catch sight of the gods or touch them. Just then the priest of Zeus cried out, "I will get garlands and oxen and prepare for sacrifice."

But Paul became greatly vexed, and shouted out, "Friends, we are not gods but mortals like yourselves. We bring you good news that you should turn away from these futile things to the living God who created the heavens and the earth, who gives you fruitful seasons and food for your bodies and fills your hearts with joy."

Showing the fickle nature of the crowd, unbelieving Jews who had come from Pisidian Antioch and Iconium stirred up the people against Paul and Barnabas. The mob went into a rage and stoned Paul, who felt the agony and pain of those he had previously committed to death. They dragged him outside the city and left him for dead. But when the disciples gathered around him, Paul arose and returned to the city. (This event is given little significance by Acts, but stoning was a certain death sentence.)

At the beginning of the first journey, Paul, Barnabas, and John Mark had sailed to the island of Cyprus. Arriving at Salamis, they began to proclaim the Gospel in the synagogues. They followed this same course throughout the island finally arriving at Paphos, home of the proconsul, Sergius Paulos. He was an intelligent and inquisitive man, who wanted to hear the evangelist's message. However, a magician named Bar-Jesus intervened and tried to turn the brothers away.

This was a most important moment, for it was the first direct challenge of the missionary journey. That is why Paul immediately confronted the magician. Filled with the Holy Spirit, he looked directly into the eyes of Bar-Jesus and exclaimed, "You scoundrel and enemy of the truth, full of deceit and evil, stop trying to obstruct the word of the Lord! And now, listen to me! The hand of the Lord is upon you and you will be unable to see for a while." The magician immediately began stumbling and groping his way around. Greatly impressed by this display of power, the proconsul listened intently to the evangelists and became a believer.

The brothers then set sail for Perga in Asia Minor. John Mark, however, left the mission at this point and returned to Jerusalem, an act which did not sit well with Paul. Traveling north from Perga, they came to Pisidian Antioch, founded by one of the generals of Alexander the Great. This city, a center of Hellenistic culture, also had an imposing position on the trade route between Ephesus and the Cilician Gates.[1] Pisidian Antioch had a number of liberal minded Jews, who had been settled there by the Seleucid kings for business and political purposes. This group of Jews welcomed Paul and Barnabas to their synagogue and were open to the Gospel. The Book of Acts records one of Paul's most important evangelical speeches.[2]

The brothers were invited to speak again the next sabbath at

---

[1] A series of narrow passages between the Taurus mountains leading to Tarsus and beyond.
[2] This speech given in a synagogue of Pisidian Antioch is recorded at the end of the book.

which time a large part of the city turned out. The more conservative Jews, however, were filled with jealousy and spoke against the Gospel. Paul and Barnabas both answered, saying that they had gone to the Jews first. But since they indicated they were unworthy of eternal life, they would go to the Gentiles, for the Lord had instructed them,

> *"I have set you to be a light for the Gentiles,*
> *so that you may bring salvation to the ends of*
> *the earth."[3]*

On hearing this, the Gentiles rejoiced and many became believers, causing the Gospel to spread throughout the region. The unbelieving Jews, however, stirred up some of the leading citizens against the evangelists, and they were driven out of the area. Acts records that they shook the dust off their feet in protest and traveled on to Iconium. They were very joyful, however, knowing that good seed had been planted.

They were received more warmly in Iconium, where the Lord enabled them to do signs and wonders in his name. Again the unbelieving Jews stirred up the Gentiles and influenced their rulers to harm them. They got wind of this attempt and fled to Lystra, where at first they were believed to be Pagan gods as described above. However in these cities as well as the next, Derbe, many disciples both Jews and Greeks were brought to the Lord. This all happened in spite of the opposition of unbelieving Jews.

On their return journey Paul and Barnabas visited each of the new churches, encouraging the members and appointing elders. With fasting and prayer, they entrusted each congregation to the

---

[3] Is. 42:6; 49:6.

Lord. They then made the long trip south to Perga, where they spoke the word before reaching the coast and sailing back to Antioch. Upon arriving, they called the church together and related the successful mission which had opened the door of faith to the Gentiles.

The churches Paul established met primarily in private homes, although from time to time several house churches met together in a larger setting. The church to Paul had no identification with a building—instead whenever or wherever believers met together, that constituted the church of God. On the other hand, isolated individuals could not be the church. An assembly had to take place for worship and mutual encouragement and assistance.

Although Paul appointed elders for each congregation, there is no indication that anyone in the church had a priestly function. Each worship service, however, probably involved the Lord's Supper or the Eucharist. Paul's strong criticism (1st Corinthians 11:17) of the way the Lord's Supper was conducted could have led (much later) to a "priest" being in charge, so communion could be celebrated in an appropriate manner.

In 1st Corinthians 12, Paul calls the church the body of Christ. "Now, you are the body of Christ and individually members of it. And God has appointed in the church first apostles, second prophets, third teachers, then workers of miracles, then healers, helpers, administrators, speakers in various kinds of tongues."[4] He compares the church to a human body with each member

---

[4] 1 Cor. 12:27,28 RSV.

(eye, ears, hands, nose, etc) contributing its own part, diverse but unified. Each individual member is needed to make the body function properly.

Paul also strongly indicates that each church was a charismatic fellowship, a union in which God's gifts to individual members are exercised for the good of the body. Paul connects these gifts with God, the Holy Spirit. Not all the gifts were spectacular like prophecy and tongues. Some were, as indicated above, helpers, administrators, and teachers. The more spectacular ones had to be tested by the community. And not all were spontaneous. Some were planned and some were spontaneously inspired by the Holy Spirit. The listing of the charisms was not meant to be complete, and the final testing was whether they built up or served the body of Christ.

An important aspect of these concepts of Paul was that the church was meant to be served by *all* its members and not run or tended to by a minority. The body of Christ could not function well without the participation of all its members. "For just as the body is one and has many members, and all the members of the body, though many, are one body, so it is with Christ. For by one Spirit we were all baptized into one body—Jews or Greeks, slaves or free—and all were made to drink of one Spirit. For the body does not consist of one member but of many. If the foot should say, 'Because I am not a hand I do not belong to the body,' that would not make it any less a part of the body."[5]

It is ironic that one of Paul's strongest warning to the church was the avoidance of *strife*. He writes in Corinthians, "For ye

---

[5] 1st Cor. 12:-15 RSV.

are yet carnal: for whereas there is among you envying and strife, and divisions, are ye not carnal, and walk as men?"[6] The church through the ages has suffered from this weakness. The abandoning of fundamental beliefs handed down by the apostles and church fathers has always been a legitimate reason for separation in the Body of Christ, but too often superficial issues have also divided Christians.

The church has evolved in many ways since the days of Paul, some simply made necessary out of practicality. It is, however, still important for the church today to study the methods of the early Christian community—especially the church at Antioch. The church community was basically the *life* of each member. Nothing was more important than the Body of Christ, and if necessary everything else had to take second place and even be sacrificed for the Body. It is no wonder that the early church grew and expanded in hostile cultures practicing Paul's important principles.

---

[6] 1st Cor. 3:3 KJV.

6

The Judaizers Oppose Paul And Barnabas

In Jerusalem the atmosphere in the great room had become very tense. Several of the disciples of Antioch including Paul and Barnabas had gone to Jerusalem to explain the planting of predominantly Gentile churches. The Judaizers were Pharisee believers who had accepted Jesus but held out for the whole law of Moses, including circumcision. Learned rabbis and Jewish scholars, representing the Judaizers, used their interpretation of scripture in an eloquent fashion. It was their contention that unless Gentile Christians submitted to circumcision and pledged to follow the law of Moses, they could not be saved. They had made an excellent case. The fate of the Gentile mission hung in the balance.

When Peter rose up to speak, the room became very silent. "My brothers, you remember that it was I who was called by God to carry the Gospel to a Gentile household. After I preached the Gospel to them, they received the Holy Spirit just as we did. Now, why do you ask that we put a burden upon them that neither we nor our ancestors could bear? We will be saved by the grace of our Lord Jesus just as they will."

Next Barnabas and Paul in turn spoke of all the wonders God had done through them among the Gentiles. Finally, all eyes turned to James, the brother of Jesus, to whom the risen Lord had appeared. Paul anxiously wondered which side the acknowledged leader of the church in Jerusalem would come down on. James began, "My brothers, you have heard Peter relate how a Gentile household was looked upon favorably by God. This agrees with the words of the prophets:

> *'After this I will return, and I will rebuild the dwelling of David, which has fallen; from its ruins I will rebuild it and I will set it up, so that all other people may seek the Lord—even all the Gentiles, over whom my name has been called. Thus says the Lord, who has been making these things known from long ago'*[1]

"In my judgment, we should not make it difficult for the Gentiles who are turning to God. Instead, we should send a letter telling them to abstain from things polluted by idols, from sexual immorality, from eating the meat of strangled animals and from tasting blood."

The assembly backed their leader and made the decision to

---

[1] Amos 9:11 and Jer. 12:15.

send Judas Barsabas and Silas together with Paul and Barnabas to Antioch to deliver a letter spelling out the Jerusalem Council's decision. When the brothers delivered the letter to the church in Antioch, there was much rejoicing. Some of the joy was premature, however, because the Judaizers, while outwardly accepting the Council's decision, were not really convinced. They would continue to hound Paul throughout his ministry, trying to teach new Christians a different way, *another gospel*. Their opposition would become a real challenge to Paul, whom they never grew to trust.

Paul's ire at the Judaizers would rise to a sharp pitch in his letter to the Galatians. He writes that if you want to be justified by the law, you have cut yourselves off from Christ, fallen from grace. He further writes, "For through the Spirit, by faith, we eagerly wait for the hope of righteousness. For in Christ Jesus neither circumcision nor un-circumcision counts for anything, the only thing that counts is faith working through love."[2] Paul further blasts the persons who were trying to confuse the Galatians and ends the passage with the wish that those who were unsettling them would castrate themselves.

It was understandable that the unbelieving Jews fought Paul's missionary efforts. The opposition of the Judaizers is more difficult to comprehend. They believed in Jesus, but still maintained that circumcision and following the whole law of Moses was necessary for salvation.

---

[2] Gal. 5:5,6 NRSV.

Paul did not negate the law, but called it a disciplinarian until the promised Christ should come. He taught that circumcision and the law could save no one, that no one could actually keep all the law. Faith in Christ, however, could save, could change minds and hearts, clear one's conscience, and lead to a full life in the Holy Spirit. This doctrine came to be called *justification by faith* and has been attested to throughout the centuries by countless lives changed by faith in Christ.

The importance of Paul's theology was demonstrated by the Reformation. It was Martin Luther who upon reading and contemplating Paul's letters and St. Augustine's writings, proclaimed that we are *justified by faith.* In Romans Paul writes words to this effect: since all have sinned and have fallen short of God's glory, we are now justified by his grace as a gift. This gift comes through the redemption that is in Jesus Christ, whom God set forth to be a sacrifice of atonement by his blood made effective through faith. God, himself, is righteous, and he justifies those who have faith in Jesus. We therefore hold that a person is *justified by faith apart from the law.*

Paul further makes his point by reaching back into Old Testament scripture to the patriarch Abraham. Abraham was complaining to the Lord about being childless. A slave born in Abraham's house was to become his heir.[3] And the word of the Lord came to Abraham, "That man will not be you heir. Your own son will be your heir."

Then the Lord brought Abraham outside and said to him, "Look at the sky, and number the stars, if you are able." Then

---

[3] This slave became Abraham's most trusted servant and according to custom would become his heir if Abraham continued childless.

He said to him, "So shall your descendants be." And he believed the Lord, and He reckoned it to him as righteousness. This occurred before the sign of circumcision had been given to Abraham and also happened several hundred years before the law of Moses. Thus the *promise* came first.[4] The Lord also promised that Abraham's seed would bless many nations.

And so Paul writes:

"He (Abraham) did not weaken in faith when he considered his own body, which was already as good as dead (for he was about a hundred years old.), or when he considered the barrenness of Sarah's womb. No distrust made him waver concerning the promise of God, being fully convinced that God was able to do what he had promised. Therefore his faith 'was reckoned to him as righteousness.' Now the words, 'it was reckoned to him' were written not for his sake alone, but for ours also. It will be reckoned to us who believe in him who raised Jesus our Lord from the dead, who was handed over to death for our trespasses and raised for our justification. Therefore, since we are justified by faith, we have peace with God through our Lord Jesus Christ, through whom we have obtained access to his grace in which we stand, and we boast in our hope of sharing the glory of God."[5]

Today this type of faith is relatively rare. Instead of Pagan "gods" and Judaizers, there are others today who resist the faith. Among them are secular rationalists and naturalists who have an inordinate influence on our culture. Some Darwinists tend to make a religion of their secular beliefs. They somehow discount

---

[4] Based on Gen. 15:3-6.
[5] Rom. 4: 19-25 NRSV (my parenthesis).

41

the latest discoveries in biochemistry indicating intelligent design.[6] And even though most scientists recognize some degree of evolution *within* major species, no fossils have been found showing intermediate steps *between* major species. This secular rationalist and naturalist influence upon our schools, colleges and universities is almost universal and results in teaching a materialistic view of life.[7] Thus we are stuck with one of the "sacred cows" of our culture, which prejudicially resists the theory of intelligent design.

---

[6] See *Darwinism under the Microscope* by James P. Gills, M.D. and Tom Woodward, Ph.D. , Lake Mary, Fla., Charisma House, 2002.

[7] There are some Christians who accept Darwin's theory of evolution, but maintain that God used this method to bring about the fullness of creation.

7

Second Missionary Journey Success And Hardship

Back in Antioch Paul and Barnabas were again enjoying the fellowship of the church. The congregation was thriving and was led by prophets, teachers, and evangelists. Paul could have been content to stay in this Spirit-filled fellowship. But deep inside he knew his commission was not fully accomplished; his thoughts kept shifting back to the newly planted churches. He wondered how they were faring, and he believed they might need encouragement and direction.

Paul's Second Missionary Journey

Used by permission of Biblical Studies Press

44

Barnabas agreed that they should undertake another missionary journey beginning with the new churches. But he said to Paul, "John Mark has matured greatly since he left us in Pamphilia. He has worked diligently for the church and shows many attributes of the Holy Spirit. I believe him to be completely trustworthy—a valuable assistant on our journey."

Paul did not reply at first as his mind raced quickly over Mark's abrupt departure on the first journey. He then replied, "We cannot be sure about Mark;[1] he is still young and unproven. Our journey could be long and difficult—even subject to hostile opposition and abuse."

"I accept full responsibility for him, for I am confident of his commitment and courage," Barnabas asserted.

But Paul was not to be persuaded and the difference of opinion led to a parting of the ways for the two old friends and Gospel warriors. Barnabas took Mark, his cousin, with him and sailed for Cyprus, while Paul was left to choose his coworker from among the brothers.

Silas at this time was a member of the church at Antioch. He had been among the first Christian leaders in Jerusalem and was much respected and trusted by the saints of both Antioch and Jerusalem. He was well educated and considered a prophet and eloquent preacher. In addition he was probably a Roman citizen,[2] and had been one of the delegation sent to Antioch with the decision of the Jerusalem Council. This was the mettle of the companion Paul was looking for. So Paul selected Silas, and after receiving the brothers' blessing, headed for Asia Minor.

---

[1] Later in Paul's ministry, Mark became a devoted friend and associate. See Philemon 1:24.
[2] Acts 16:37.

Paul was both elated and thankful when he found the churches well and growing. The evangelists delivered the Jerusalem Council's decision, which was received with much rejoicing.

In Lystra they met a young disciple named Timothy. His mother was a Jewish believer, but his father was Greek. The believers in Lystra and Iconium spoke highly of him. So Paul, after becoming fully acquainted, recruited him for missionary work. Before starting out, Paul took Timothy and had him circumcised because of the Jews, who knew that his father was a Greek. This act might seem contrary to Paul's position on circumcision, but he did it to avoid any brand the Jews might place on Timothy—such as regarding him as a half-breed. They then headed northwest since the Holy Spirit had forbidden them to speak the Gospel in Asia.[3]

Traveling a long way through sparsely populated areas, they finally reached the border of Bithynia, but the Spirit of Jesus would not let them go in, so they journeyed down to Troas on the Aegean Sea. After finding lodging, the three evangelists were getting ready to turn in for the night. Since Paul and Silas both had benefited from a Hellenist education and were familiar with Homer, the subject of the Trojan War naturally came up. Silas spoke first, "While we are so close, I would like to see the ruins of Troy[4]. I'm told the site is only a few miles north of here."

---

[3] In the book of Acts, the writer describes Asia as Ephesus and the surrounding cities where Paul later preached.

[4] 2000 years ago there was most likely still an awareness of the location of Troy. Much later, in the 19th century it was discovered and excavated by the German amateur archeologist, Schliemann.

46

"Perhaps we'll have that opportunity," said Paul, "while we await the direction of the Spirit."

Timothy listened intently as a discussion ensued involving the personalities and plots of the ancient Greek army as they tried to overthrow Troy. The conversation trailed off into a sound sleep for the three travel weary men. But for Paul, his dream did not include Helen of Troy, Achilles, Hector, or any of the other mythical heroes of Homer's classic. Instead, he clearly saw the vision of a Macedonian man pleading for the three evangelists to come across the sea and help them. Consequently, in the morning Paul told Silas of the dream and concluded, "I believe the Lord is calling us to preach the Gospel in Macedonia. We should cross the sea at once and go to them."

"I cannot oppose the vision. Troy will have to wait." Silas agreed.

Crossing the sea by boat, they[5] arrived in Macedonia and traveled to the capital city of Philippi, named after the father of Alexander the Great. The evangelists found proselytes by the river where a place of prayer had been established, and Paul met Lydia, a worshiper of God. She was a prominent business woman dealing in purple cloth. The Lord opened her heart to Paul, and after she and her household were all baptized, she persuaded the brothers to stay at her home. This was an important occasion because the Gospel was preached in Philippi for the first time in Europe.

---

[5] The subject "we" is used for a time in Acts indicating that Luke, the physician and author of Acts, was in their company. He appears later in the narrative when the subject "we" is used again.

The marketplace in Philippi was teeming with people, some shopping and others milling about, greeting friends. Children were playing chase with each other occasionally bumping into adults. There were small groups of laborers waiting to be hired out. Paul and his companions were wending their way through, going to the place of prayer by the river. Suddenly, they were confronted by the slave girl who had followed them for several days.

"These men are servants of the Most High God who are proclaiming to you the way of salvation," shouted the girl who had brought her owners much money by fortune telling. She apparently had a spirit of divination, and she kept following the brothers, repeating her message at every opportunity. Finally, Paul grew very annoyed. He turned and sternly addressed the spirit, "In the name of Jesus Christ, I order you to come out of her." Immediately the spirit left.

When the girl's owners realized their hope of making money was gone, they dragged Paul and Silas through the marketplace to the authorities. Once before the magistrates, the owners exclaimed, "These men are Jews and are advocating practices unlawful for Romans to adopt." The crowd concurred, yelling many accusations.

After giving Paul and Silas a severe flogging, they were thrown into prison and fastened securely with their feet in stocks. That could have been a time of defeat and discouragement. But instead, about midnight songs were heard in the prison as Paul and Silas began singing hymns of praise and thanksgiving. All the prisoners were listening attentively.

Suddenly a deafening noise exploded throughout the prison

and the ground began to shake violently. The earthquake opened all the doors and unfastened all the chains and stocks. The jailor, fearing all the prisoners would escape, prepared to fall on his sword, but Paul shouted, "Don't harm yourself. We are all here." After washing and binding up the wounds of the evangelists, the jailor asked what he should do in order to be saved. Paul replied, "Believe in the Lord Jesus, and you will be saved." The jailor and all his household were then baptized.

When morning arrived, the magistrates sent word to the jailor to let the brothers go. But Paul commented, "They have whipped us in public, uncondemned Roman citizens, and thrown us into prison. Let them come down themselves and take us out." When this was reported back to the officials, they became frightened, hastened to the jail and apologized to Paul and Silas. They then released the evangelists and pleaded for them to leave the city.

After leaving Philippi, Paul, Silas, and Timothy preached in Thessalonica, where they were hounded by unbelieving Jews. They then arrived at Beroea, where they were eagerly received by the Jews, who searched the scriptures daily to prove the truth of the message. Finally, the Jews of Thessalonica arrived and harrassed the brothers, causing Paul to leave the area and head for Athens. Timothy and Silas stayed behind to assist the new churches. They planned to join Paul later.

8

Alone In a City Of Multiple Gods and Philosophies

When Paul left Silas and Timothy with the believers in Beroea and headed for Athens, he must have felt very lonesome. He was still young enough to have an abundance of energy and stamina, but he had been stoned, whipped, put into prison and run out of almost every city. He missed his traveling companions and wondered what unknown tribulations lay ahead.

Walking into the great citadel of daily debates, pagan gods, and world-view philosophies, he hoped and prayed that someone would listen to his Gospel. As he entered the city, he passed monument after monument, temple after temple, dedicated to various pagan gods. He gazed upon the Acropolis with its beautiful, gleaming buildings such as the Parthenon, Temple of the Wingless Victory and others. Athens was truly a spectacular city.

At least he could speak the Greek language, and he soon inquired and found the synagogue where he began arguing with the Jews on the sabbath. During other days he spoke in the marketplace to anyone who would listen. He even attracted the attention of some Stoic and Epicurean philosophers with whom he debated. They had no background for understanding Paul, but they were curious, and they soon persuaded Paul to speak to the Areopagus, a council of philosophers who normally met on a hill called by the same name. The hill had a spectacular view, overlooking Athens and situated close to the Acropolis.

"So Paul, standing in the middle of the Areopagus, said: 'Men of Athens, I perceive that in every way you are very religious. For as I passed along, and observed the objects of your worship, I found also an altar with this inscription, *To an unknown god.* What you therefore worship as unknown, this I proclaim to you. The God who made the world and everything in it, being Lord of heaven and earth, does not live in shrines made by man, nor is he served by human hands, as though he needed anything, since he himself gives to all men life and breath and everything.

'And he made from one (man) every nation of men to live on all the face of the earth, having determined allotted periods and the boundaries of their habitation, that they should seek God, in the hope that they might feel after him and find him. Yet he is

Paul addresses the Areopagus

not far from each one of us, for *In him we live and move and have our being*; as even some of your poets have said, *For we are indeed his offspring.*....The times of ignorance God overlooked, but now he commands all men everywhere to repent because he has fixed a day on which he will judge the world in righteousness by a man whom he has appointed, and of this he has given assurance to all men by raising him from the dead.' "[1]

The reaction to this speech was mixed with some scoffing and others saying, "We will hear you again." A few, however, believed and formed the nucleus of a future church in Athens.

This speech (the above being a summary), to a sophisticated and educated audience of debaters and philosophers, was something of a masterpiece. Paul was a stranger with no standing or following. However, he knew the temperament and mind of the well versed men of Athens and their pagan understanding. So with his Hellenist background, he was able to deliver a believable message and as a result won a number of converts. This took courage, faith, and guidance of the Holy Spirit. *God, grant to us in this day that, surrounded by unbelief and scoffers, we might stand on the rock of the Gospel and show our faith to be as solid as Paul's. Amen.*

Paul did not stay long in Athens. And even though he had presented himself well against seasoned debaters and philosophers, he left with a sense of disappointment.

---

[1] Acts 17: 22-31 RSV (my parenthesis).

He entered Achaia[2] and headed for Corinth, the capital city. The year was 51 or 52 AD when Gallio was governor. Corinth was a rich, cosmopolitan port city, situated on the narrow isthmus called the Peloponnesus which separates the north of Greece and Europe from the south. On each side of the isthmus were deep water ports. Some smaller vessels were transported on tracks from one port to the other, saving a long and dangerous voyage around southern Greece. As could be expected, Corinth was morally corrupt. Seamen and businessmen of several cultures spent their nights there in licentious pleasures.

Paul also entered Corinth alone. However two events made his long stay there most encouraging. First, he found a friendly Jewish couple, Aquila and Priscilla. Because they were of the same tent making trade as Paul, he stayed with them and they soon became devoted disciples. Later, the Lord spoke to him, saying, "Speak, and do not be afraid. I will let no one harm you. I have many people in this city."

Many adventures awaited Paul in Corinth. As was his custom, he went first to the synagogue, where he argued every sabbath that Jesus was the Messiah. Silas and Timothy arrived at this time. And although Paul made many converts, both Jews and Greeks, the unbelieving Jews finally drove him out of the synagogue. Again in disgust, Paul spoke his intention of taking the Gospel to the Gentiles.

Not to be outdone, Paul began lecturing in a God worshiper's house which was next door to the synagogue. In an extraordinary and ironic turn of events, Paul even converted

---

[2] The southern half of ancient Greece.

Crispus, the ruler of the synagogue, together with many others. The Jews and the Greeks were finding in the Gospel a sense of personal fulfillment which could not be found in Greek philosophy or even Judaism.

Finally the unbelieving Jews attacked Paul and brought him before the tribunal. Sosthenes, a synagogue official, presented the case against Paul ending with the words, "This man is persuading people to worship God in a manner contrary to the law." But just as Paul was preparing to defend himself, the proconsul Gallio surprisingly declared, "It seems to me this case is about Jewish laws and customs and therefore has no standing before this tribunal. The case is dismissed." At that ruling, the people seized Sosthenes and began beating him in plain sight of Gallio, who refused to pay any attention whatsoever to this unexpected turnaround.

In all, Paul spent about 18 productive months in Corinth, establishing a flourishing church there. He then bade farewell to the church and set sail for Jerusalem, stopping briefly at Ephesus, where he left Aquila and Priscilla to begin teaching the word of the Lord.

The churches established by Paul on his missionary journeys were planted in hostile cultures. In addition, they all encountered various internal problems just as the churches of today. News of these problems came to Paul either by letter or by personal messenger. Paul replied with letters of his own which make up what we know about Paul's theology. That is what makes the letters so important. They are Paul's answer to real problems faced by the first missionary congregations—problems much the same as the Christian church faces today.

The letters show Paul's extraordinary grasp of the Gospel, his great intellectual prowess, and the reason he is still called the foremost theologian of the church. Some of the main aspects of Paul's faith, as recorded in the letters, will be described as the rest of Paul's amazing story is told. These aspects are not only important to today's church but also to a world in great need of the Gospel.

As a Jew and even a Pharisee, Paul used parts of the Hebrew scripture throughout his letters. His understanding of the plight of human beings is closely linked to the Genesis account of mankind's beginning and fall. In the letter to the Corinthians he writes, "For since death came through a human being (Adam)..." and "for as in Adam all die ..." and in Romans, "Therefore, just as sin came into the world through one man, and death came through sin, and so death spread to all because all have sinned...Yet death exercised dominion from Adam to Moses, even over those whose sins were not like the transgression of Adam..." And again in Romans, "...all have sinned and fallen short of the glory of God..."

In Romans Paul makes it clear all should have recognized God even though he is invisible. This was made possible through mankind's observance of the creation of the world showing forth God's eternal power and divine nature. However they did not honor God or give him thanks. "Therefore God gave them up in the lusts of their hearts to impurity, to the degrading of their bodies among themselves, because *they exchanged the truth about God for a lie and worshiped and served the creature rather than the Creator, who is blessed forever! Amen."* [3]

This indictment of humanity was necessary and generally accurate. The fallen state of mankind was definitely in need of the saving grace of God. But what about today; does this passage strike some familiar notes concerning American culture? And even though there are many who fear and worship God, some facets of our culture appear to be moving in the direction Paul so vividly described. Paul's message to us today might be much the same. A Savior is needed. And that Savior is not some vain imagination of mankind such as Superman; nor is he an overblown, charismatic political leader. Rather, he is God's own Son, sent to humanity to fulfill God's purpose of redemption and salvation.

---

[3] Romans 1:24, 25 NRSV.

9

The Rigors Of Apostleship

"I am a better minister of Christ than these 'super-apostles.' I have labored far harder, faced more imprisonments. I have suffered more beatings—I received thirty nine lashes five times at the hands of the Jews. I was beaten with rods three times. I was even stoned and left for dead. I have experienced three shipwrecks and was a day and a night adrift at sea. On my journeys I faced danger from robbers, danger from my own people, danger from Gentiles, danger in the city and danger in the wilderness, in strenuous work and in hardship, through many sleepless nights, in hunger and thirst, often without food, cold and with exposure. In addition to all this, I felt the daily pressure and anxiety for all the churches"[1] Paul wrote to the Corinthians, defending himself against the Judaizers who were trying to introduce *another gospel.*

Today we tend to think lightly of Paul's journeys. We are used to traveling by car, airplane or fast train. In Paul's day the general mode of transportation on land was by foot or at best by camel or horse. A distance of 150 miles generally took about one week. Today by car we can make it in about three hours. In addition, there was little or no presence of security. People traveling on roads through the countryside were often attacked by robbers. There were no first-aid stations or hospitals. Falling ill on a long trip could be fatal or in any case most debilitating.

Travel at sea on a sailing ship was almost as hazardous. There were no weather forecasts, no communications, and what seemed to be fine weather could quickly turn into a dangerous storm. Each one of Paul's journeys involved hundreds of miles, many by land and some by sea.

But the distances traveled were not the greatest danger. Paul was taking an unknown religion into pagan countries, which had hundreds of years of historic pagan culture. In addition, he was frequently attacked by his own people, the Jews, who were deeply rooted in their own religious beliefs and customs. When he wasn't offending them, he was offending pagan gods or goddesses and the people who believed in them.

---

[1] Based on 2nd Cor, 11:23-28.

If a comparison had to be made today, imagine a group of believers trying to take Christianity into Muslim countries. It would be constantly life threatening. At least the mode of travel (perhaps out of this world) would be much faster.

All this goes to speak of Paul's character—determination, courage, dedication and faith. In addition there was the overwhelming commission given to him by Jesus, a mandate which would afford him no pause or rest. He was a person who would never quit, never give in, in spite of all the hardships and punishments he faced, and in spite of the enormous odds stacked against him.

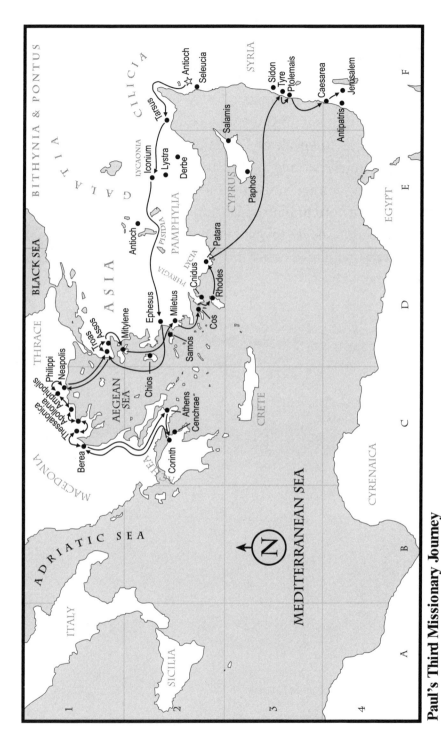

Paul's Third Missionary Journey

According to the story, Paul went from Tarsus to all four cities of Derbe, Lystra, Iconium and Antioch before proceeding to Ephesus.

Used by permission of Biblical Studies Press

10

Third Missionary Journey
Ephesus, A Center For Asia

Paul's second journey had ended with his return to Jerusalem and then to Antioch. But after a short respite, the Spirit led Paul to promptly begin his third missionary journey. This time we are not told who his disciple-companion was; it could have been Silas, or more likely several disciples chosen from the new churches as he journeyed. He left by land, traveling around the Mediterranean to Tarsus, up through the mountain pass to the cities of Derbe, Lystra, Iconium, Pisidian Antioch, and west to Ephesus. The time was circa 55 AD.

At the time of Paul, Ephesus was one of the most important cities in the Roman Empire with a population of more than 200,000. It was a center of trade and commerce, being a port city by virtue of its position on a river not far from the Mediterranean. Its great theater, now excavated by archaeologists, seated about 25,000, and its temple dedicated to Artemis was several times larger than the Parthenon in Athens and just as beautiful and ornate.

It is certain that Paul had a joyful reunion with Aquila and Priscilla and stayed with them again. Paul also found some disciples who had been baptized with John's baptism only. Upon being baptized in the name of the Lord Jesus, Paul laid his hands on them, and they began speaking in tongues and prophesying.

Paul then entered the synagogue and on every sabbath for three months spoke out boldly concerning the kingdom of God. When some of the Jews spoke evil about the Way, Paul left them, taking his disciples with him. He then lectured for two years in the lecture hall of Tyrannus. During that time many residents of the surrounding towns, who occasionally visited Ephesus, heard the word of the Lord.

This was an important time for Christianity, for later when tradition tells us that the Apostle John preached and was prominent in Ephesus, many people in seven Asian cities had already been converted by Paul. These are the seven cities cited in Revelation[1]. Also while Paul was in Ephesus, he wrote 1st Corinthians, one of his most important letters and theological tracts in which he sends greetings from Aquila and Priscilla and the church which met in their house.

In Ephesus, Paul did many acts of power in the name of the Lord Jesus. He healed the sick and delivered many from evil

---

[1] Smyrna, Pergamum, Thyatira, Sardis, Philadelphia, Laodicea, Ephesus.

spirits. It was said that when aprons or handkerchiefs touched his skin, they could be taken to the sick who recovered. These miracles greatly impressed the people and added many to the Way

An unusual and bizarre event occurred in Ephesus when some Jewish exorcists began to use the name of Jesus in their practice of exorcising evil spirits. Seven sons of a Jewish high priest were practicing exorcism on a possessed man. When they called upon the name of Jesus, the evil spirit answered, "I know Jesus and Paul, but who the devil are you?" The possessed man threw himself upon them, overcame them all and ran them out of his house, naked and wounded.

The story of this act spread all over Ephesus and the surrounding countryside. It resulted in even more respect and honor for Paul and his associates. A number of those who practiced magic even brought their magic arts books and burned them in the sight of all.

Demetrius was a decent man and a very good silversmith. He was not wealthy, but worked hard at his trade and made a good living. He had a wife and two children and lived in a respectable neighborhood of Ephesus. He really held nothing against the evangelists, but when Paul's preaching began to attract Gentiles away from the worship of Artemis, his business began to suffer. One of the most popular items of his trade was a silver shrine of Artemis.

Seeing this trend begin to hurt his and other silversmiths' business, Demetrius called the artisans together. He made an impassioned speech claiming that Paul had turned a large number of people away from the worship of Artemis. He said, "And there is danger not only that this trade of ours might come into disrepute, but also that the temple of the great goddess Artemis may count for nothing, and that she may even he deposed from her magnificence, she whom all Asia and the world worship."[2]

When they heard this, the artisans became enraged and began to shout, "Great is Artemis of the Ephesians." They took to the streets with this shouting, exciting many citizens, who rushed together and hurried to the house of Aquila and Priscilla, bent on doing away with Paul.

The mob surrounded the house and demanded that Paul come out. Over his strenuous objections, the couple hid Paul in a small cellar concealed by a rug just as the angry men burst into the house. Not finding Paul, they dragged Gaius and Aristarchus[3] to the great town theater. There was much confusion and some did not know why they had come together. Paul wanted to leave the house and go into the crowd, but his friends and disciples would not let him. In the theater Alexander motioned with his hand to try and talk in the defense of the evangelists, but when the crowd recognized that he was a Jew, they shouted even louder, "Great is Artemis of the Ephesians!" This went on for two hours.

Finally the town clerk, who apparently commanded great respect, quieted down the mob. He argued that there was not a person there who did not know that Ephesus was the temple

---

[2] Acts 19:27 RSV.

[3] Traveling companions of Paul.

keeper of the great Artemis and of the sacred stone which fell from the sky. Further, he stated that such things cannot be contradicted, and that the men brought there by the mob were not blasphemers of Artemis.

He reasoned that if anyone had a complaint, it could be brought before the courts and proconsuls and properly settled. Anything further could be settled in the regular assembly. And he warned the crowd about being charged with rioting, a serious matter with the Romans. He then dismissed those assembled.

This unusual event in Ephesus indicates just how volatile the situation could turn against Paul and his disciples. It was typical of the dangers he faced in every city where he preached the Gospel. In Romans (16:4) Paul thanks Aquila and Priscilla[4] for risking their lives for him.

Paul makes one unusual reference to Ephesus in 1st Corinthians when he writes, "Why are we also in danger every hour? I affirm, brethren, by the boasting in you which I have in Christ Jesus our Lord, I die daily. If from human motives I fought with wild beasts at Ephesus, what does it profit me?[5] In Acts there is no reference to Paul actually fighting with wild beast in Ephesus, so the passage is interpreted to mean that Paul is calling his adversaries in Ephesus "wild beasts." In the riot described above, it might not be inappropriate to do so.

---

[4] When Paul first met Aquila and Priscilla in Corinth, they had been run out of Rome by Emperor Claudius. Romans indicates they had returned to Rome.

[5] 1st Cor. 15:30-32a NASB.

When the time had come for Paul to leave Ephesus, he called the disciples together and gave them much encouragement. He then said his farewell and sailed for Macedonia, where he visited the churches, enlivening the congregations and taking up a collection for the poor Christians of Jerusalem.

While traveling through Macedonia, Paul wrote his 2nd letter to the Corinthians. He then entered Greece, visiting each church and making further collections for the poor of Jerusalem. In Corinth he wrote his fullest theological tract, the letter to the Romans.

He was about to sail for Syria when a plot against him by the Jews was discovered. It was decided that he should return through Macedonia and meet the other disciples in Troas. This was another indication of the hatred felt by traditional Jews against Paul; it was not to be the last. About this time the narrative in Acts shifts in its presentation with the word "we" becoming the usual subject, indicating that Luke, the physician and author of Acts, had again joined the brothers.

While waiting for a ship to sail from Troas, Paul held a service with the disciples and local Christians on the first day of the week. Showing his usual inexhaustible knowledge of the Gospel and energized by the Spirit, Paul taught and held discussions with the group until midnight. One young man, sitting in an open window, fell asleep and dropped three stories to the ground. The brothers rushed down to help him. Believing he was dead, they were very disconsolate. But Paul went down and taking the youth's body in his arms said, "Do not worry.

His life is still in him." Then Paul went inside, ate supper and continued his discussion until dawn. The young man left with the others who were very comforted.

On the return trip to Jerusalem, the ship put in at Miletus, where Paul sent a message to the elders of the church in Ephesus, asking them to meet him. Assembling on the shore, Paul addressed them with a poignant and moving farewell: "You yourselves know how I lived among you the entire time from the first day that I set foot in Asia, serving the Lord with all humility and with tears, enduring the trials that came to me through the plots of the Jews. I did not shrink from doing any thing helpful, proclaiming the message to you and teaching you publicly and from house to house, as I testified to both Jews and Greeks about repentance toward God and faith toward our Lord Jesus.

"And now, as a captive to the Spirit, I am on my way to Jerusalem, not knowing what will happen to me there, except that the Holy Spirit testifies to me in every city that imprisonment and persecutions are waiting for me. But I do not count my life of any value to myself, if only I may finish my course and the ministry that I received from the Lord Jesus, to testify to the good news of God's grace. And I know that none of you, among whom I have gone about proclaiming the kingdom, will ever see my face again....

"I did not shrink from declaring to you the whole purpose of God. Keep watch over yourselves and over all the flock, of which the Holy Spirit has made you overseers, to shepherd the church of God that he obtained with the blood of his own Son. I know that after I am gone, savage wolves will come in among you, not sparing the flock...Therefore be alert remembering that for three years I did not cease night or day to warn everyone with tears.

"And now I commend you to God and to the message of his grace to give you the inheritance among all who are sanctified…You know for yourselves that I worked with my own hands to support myself and my companions. In all this I have given you an example that by such work we must support the weak, remembering the words of the Lord Jesus, for he himself said, 'It is more blessed to give than to receive.' "[6]

Then they all knelt down and prayed. There was much weeping and embracing Paul, grieving that he had said they would not see him again. A very deeply moving relationship had developed between Paul and the Ephesian elders. Their lives had been changed by Paul; he had become their father in Christ, and they shared a special love for him.

At this point in his life, Paul was beginning to feel his age and the many scars caused by his ministry for Christ. His black beard had turned white, and flecks of silver were beginning to show in his receding hair. The fast steady gait, which strained his companions to keep up, had slowed, and he walked with a slight limp. Secondly, he was directly facing his mortality, knowing the warnings of the Holy Spirit concerning his return to Jerusalem. He was also seriously beginning to question whether he would be alive at the return of Christ, the Parousia.

---

[6] Acts 20:18b-35 NRSV.

11

The Humanity Of Paul

Paul with all his intellect and Holy Spirit guidance was not so egotistical as to think he knew it all—had all the knowledge of God's purposes and activities. "For now we see in a mirror dimly, but then face to face. Now I know in part, then I shall understand fully...."[1] This quotation from Paul's first letter to the Corinthians indicates his honesty and humility.

Paul knew that he was not nearly perfect. For he wrote in Philippians, "...that I may know him and the power of his resurrection, and may share his suffering, becoming like him in

---

[1] 1st Cor. 13:12a RSV.

his death, that if possible I may obtain the resurrection from the dead. Not that I have already obtained this or am already perfect; but I press on to make it my own, because Christ Jesus has made me his own. Brethren, I do not consider that I have made it my own; but one thing I do, forgetting what lies behind and straining forward to what lies ahead, I press on toward the goal for the prize of the upward call of God in Christ Jesus."[2]

There are other instances in Paul's letters which attest to his humanity—even his weaknesses. In Romans he writes, "...we know that the law is spiritual, but I am of the flesh, sold into slavery under sin. I do not understand my own actions. For I do not do what I want, but I do the very thing I hate...For I know that nothing good dwells within me, that is in my flesh. I can will what is right but I cannot do it...So when I find it to be a law that when I want to do what is good, evil lies close at hand. For I delight in the law of God in my inmost parts, but I see in my members another law at war with the law of my mind, making me captive to the law of sin...Wretched man that I am! Who will rescue me from this body of death? Thanks be to God through Jesus Christ our Lord!"[3]

Of course this is just another affirmation of Paul's that the law cannot make us good—change our hearts, only faith in Christ can.

In 2nd Corinthians Paul writes, "...a thorn was given me in the flesh, a messenger of Satan to torment me, to keep me from being too elated. Three times I appealed to the Lord about this, that it would leave me, but he said to me, 'My grace is sufficient

---

[2] Phil. 3:10-14 RSV.
[3] Romans 7:14-25 NRSV.

for you, for power is made perfect in weakness.' So I will boast all the more gladly of my weaknesses, so that the power of Christ may dwell in me."[4]

No one really knows exactly what this thorn was. It was never revealed to us. It might have been some ailment or physical impairment. However, it can be encouraging to know that Paul had his weaknesses just as most of us. What he did in spite of those weaknesses in regard to spiritual power is the important issue. We don't have to be Superman to be good witnesses of Christ. Our power just might be greater because of our weaknesses.

There are some who believe that a patriarchal society influenced Paul and constituted one of his weaknesses. St. Paul was not married. He was married to his ministry. In his letters to the churches a number of passages have given the impression that he somehow accorded women fewer rights than men. For example, in 1st Corinthians 14:34 and 35 Paul writes, "As in all the churches of the saints, women should be silent in the churches. For they are not permitted to speak, but should be subordinate, as the law also says."[5]

At least two explanations should be examined. First, the cultures, both Greek and Hebrew, put very strict rules on women. Women in the synagogue not only had to keep quiet, they sat in a different section behind a screen from the men. Also as Paul suggests, the law disparaged talkative women.

---

[4] 2nd Corinthians 12:7b-9 NRSV.
[5] Almost the same admonition is found in 1 Tim. 2:11,12.

Paul definitely was influenced by his Jewish ancestral background.

The placement of this passage (concerning women keeping silent) comes near the close of a whole chapter which Paul devotes to keeping *good order* in church. He has just defined his rules about prophesy and speaking in tongues in church in such a way as to insure order. The sentence preceding the above reference to women is, "…God is not a god of confusion but of peace, as in all the churches of the saints."[6] All this leads to the plausible explanation that the Christian women of Corinth were exercising their freedom from the patriarchal culture a little too eagerly. Were they disrupting the good order of the service? This interpretation falls strictly within the context of the chapter.

It is possible that Paul permitted women to pray and prophesy in church[7] for in 1st Corinthians 11:5a, he writes, "…any woman who prays or prophesies with her head unveiled disgraces her head…" Of course, that brings up the question of women's hair. Again the customs of Corinth played a part.

Respectable women in that culture wore veils[8] on their heads. Prostitutes advertised themselves by wearing their long hair unveiled. Corinth was a very licentious city. As women in the street wore veils as a sign of respectability and even protection, Paul carried that custom into the Corinthian church. Also, in the Christian church in distinction from the synagogue, women sat

---

[6] 1st Cor. 14:33 NRSV.
[7] There was a difference between talking or speaking and praying or prophesying.
[8] The Greek veil and also the Hebrew veil were not long as we see in the Arab world today, but short covering only the head and shoulders.

with the men. Beautiful long hair could easily have been a distraction to many men during the service.

There can be no doubt that Paul was influenced by his great respect for Hebrew scripture including Genesis, which teaches that man came from God and that woman came from man. (God took a rib out of man to fashion woman.) Therefore, Paul writes, "But I want you to understand that Christ is the head of every man, and the husband is the head of his wife, and God is the head of Christ."[9] This was the design of relationships which Paul derived from Hebrew scripture. This pattern of order does influence Paul's views.

However, Paul was also a man far ahead of his culture and time. It is evident that women played an important role in the church. In Romans Paul writes, "I commend to you our sister, Phoebe, a deacon of the church at Cenchreae, so that you may welcome her in the Lord as is fitting for the saints, and help her in whatever she may require of you, for she has been a benefactor of many and of myself as well."[10]

To the Philippians Paul wrote: "I urge Euodia and I urge Syntyche to be of the same mind in the Lord. Yes, and I ask you also, my loyal companions, help these women, for they have struggled beside me in the work of the gospel, together with Clement and the rest of my co-workers, whose names are in the book of life."[11] And from Acts and Paul's letters we know of the important role Priscilla played in teaching the Gospel and in saving Paul's life.

In Romans Paul writes the following, "Greet Andronicus and

[9] 1st Cor. 11:3 NRSV.
[10] Rom. 16:1,2 NRSV.
[11] Phil. 4:2,3 NRSV.

Junia, my relatives who were in prison with me; they are prominent among the apostles and they were in Christ before I was."[12] And Paul goes on to list at least six more women who were prominent in the proclamation of the Gospel.

Paul is also commonly criticized for the few brief remarks he makes about slavery in 1st Corinthians, Colossians, Philemon and 1st Timothy. These remarks range all over the subject from recommending that slaves remain in their present state to a denunciation of slave traders.

Slavery in the ancient world was vastly different from today's perception. First of all, slavery was an institution universally accepted in the time of Paul. It is estimated that one person out of three in Italy was a slave.[13] These people held many different positions which ranged from work gangs to highly respected civil servants and beloved household servants. Many were better off than free persons. Many could earn money and buy back their freedom, while others were commonly given their freedom in the wills of their masters or even set free because of their devoted service.

People became slaves in various ways. Some were captured in wars; others owed debts they could not pay and sold themselves into slavery. Others were convicted of crimes. Slavery knew no particular nationality or race.

In 1st Corinthians Paul advises converted slaves to stay as

---

[12] Rom. 16:7 NRSV.
[13] *Holman Bible Dictionary*, Holman Bible Publishers 1991, p. 1286.

they are, writing that they are really slaves to Christ, just as converted free persons are.[14] He writes, "For whoever was called in the Lord as a slave is a freed person belonging to the Lord, just as whoever was free when called is a slave of Christ."[15]

Paul writes to the Colossians, "Masters, treat your slaves justly and fairly, for you know that you also have a Master in heaven."[16] In the First Letter to Timothy, Paul lists slave traders in the same category as those who kill their fathers and mothers and those who are lawless, godless and murderers and whatever else is contrary to the Gospel.

Onesimus was a slave of Philemon, who had sent him to help the imprisoned Paul. In the letter to Philemon, Paul pleads on the basis of love to Philemon to accept Onesimus back as a beloved brother and not as a slave, in other words to set him free and even take him in as part of his family. Paul writes, "So if you consider me your partner, welcome him as you would welcome me. If he has wronged you in any way, or owes you anything, charge that to my account....Yes, brother, let me have this benefit from you in the Lord! Refresh my heart in Christ. Confident of your obedience, I am writing to you, knowing that you will do even more than I say."[17]

Slavery was so much a part of life in 1 AD that no one person or group of persons could have changed it. The same principles

---

[14] Paul believed at this time that the 2nd Coming of Christ was imminent.
[15] 1st Cor. 7:22 NRSV.
[16] Col. 4:1 NRSV.
[17] Philemon 1:17,18, 20, 21 NRSV.

taught by Jesus and Paul, however, led to its demise in England and later in America and all Western countries.

Finally, in Galatians Paul makes one of his most definitive statements, "There is no longer Jew or Greek, there is no longer slave or free, there is no longer male and female, for all of you are one in Christ Jesus."[18]

Even though Paul was chosen by Christ, was filled with the Holy Spirit, and was a mystic, he was, as he told the people of Lystra, a mortal like themselves. We should celebrate the great accomplishments and theology of Paul and be content to recognize him as a human being like ourselves.

---

[18] Gal. 3:28 NRSV.

Part Two
An Evangelist In Chains

12

Paul's Understanding Of Christ
A New Creation For Mankind

It is important to review how Paul understood Jesus Christ. Perhaps it is important especially to the world of today, which is called by some, "Post Christian" or "Post Modern." In our world, human nature has not changed, but serious secular movements have tended to shape our world view. Many of these movements are gladly picked up by the media as somehow novel or new or as originated by some intellectually liberated pundit. Even in some churches "liberal theology"— preaching *another gospel*, is not only tolerated but highly publicized and accepted. Some clerical authorities are interpreting the scripture in a humanistic way and revising it in a way closer to the values of our society.

There is even the trend toward inclusive syncretism, which always excludes the unique nature of the Son of God. There is a tacit denial of the Biblical statement that Jesus Christ is *the way, the truth and the life.* Some preach that there are other ways to God—in order not to offend other religions. Bible oriented Christians believe that Christ is *God's plan* for mankind's redemption. And the Bible teaches us to love all human beings regardless of their character, religion, or race. Christians are not to pass judgment on others—that is God's prerogative.

In Philippians Paul describes Christ in this way, "...though he was in the form of God, did not count equality with God a thing to be grasped, but emptied himself, taking the form of a servant, being born in the likeness of men. And being found in human form, he humbled himself and became obedient unto death, even death on a cross. Therefore, God has highly exalted him and bestowed on him the name which is above every other name, that at the name of Jesus every knee should bow, in heaven and on earth and under the earth, and every tongue confess that Jesus Christ is Lord, to the glory of God the Father."[1]

Paul called Christ "...the image of the invisible God, the firstborn of all creation...He himself is before all things, in him all things hold together. He is the head of the body, the church,

---

[1] Phil. 2:6-11 RSV These verses are thought by some to be a pre-Pauline hymn used by Paul.

he is the beginning, the firstborn from the dead, so that he might come to have first place in everything. For in him all the fullness of God was pleased to dwell, and through him God was pleased to reconcile to himself all things, whether on earth or in heaven, by making peace through the blood of his cross."[2] And in 2nd Corinthians, "...the god of this world has blinded the minds of the unbelievers, to keep them from seeing the light of the gospel of the glory of Christ, who is the image of God."[3]

Paul believed that Christ is the truth behind and beyond all truth including science and philosophy. Paul further writes to the Colossians, "...I want their hearts to be encouraged and united in love, so that they might have all the riches of assured understanding and have the knowledge of God's mystery, that is Christ himself, in whom are hidden all the treasures of wisdom and knowledge. I am saying this so that no one may deceive you with plausible arguments....See to it that no one takes you captive through philosophy and empty deceit, according to human tradition, according to the elemental spirits of the universe and not according to Christ."[4] Humans have access to God and to salvation only through Jesus Christ, the Son of God, the sinless one, who entered the world where sin reigned in order to overcome it.

And while Paul does not enunciate the doctrine of the Trinity, he closely associates Christ with the Spirit[5] and (as pointed out

---

[2] Col. 1:15-20 NRSV.

[3] 2nd Corinthians 4;4 NRSV.

[4] Col. 2:2,3,4,8 NRSV.

[5] In Rom. 8,9 and Phil. 1:19 Paul actually uses the words, "Spirit of Christ." But in the majority of cases he uses the words, "Holy Spirit of God." The three persons of God are inseparable. God acts in Christ and Christ acts in the Holy Spirit.

above) with the Father, Himself. Pauline theology therefore stands as a bulwark against a watered down Gospel or as he called it *another gospel*. The world today and especially the church would do well to fully understand Paul's theology—a straight path toward forgiveness of sins, the life of the Spirit, the gift of eternal life, and God's righteousness.

Every human being likes to hear good news, and that is what Paul's Gospel consisted of—the good news of God in Christ Jesus. This good news speaks to the heart of those willing to listen.

The appealing aspects of Paul's Gospel were the gifts of forgiveness of sins and eternal life for all who received Christ. Then came the gift of the Holy Spirit and the capacity of loving others and following the will of God. For Paul this amazing gift of God's grace for sinners represented a new creation for humanity, an era characterized by the opening up for believers of an unlimited future of sharing in the glory of God.

"But in fact Christ has been raised from the dead, the first fruits of those who have fallen asleep. For as by a man came death, by a man has also come the resurrection of the dead. for as in Adam all die, so also in Christ shall all be made alive."[6] Paul focuses our attention on the difference between Adam (a type of original mankind) and Jesus Christ. "Therefore just as one man's trespass led to condemnation for all, so one man's act of righteousness leads to justification and life for all. For just as

---

[6] 1 Cor. 15: 20-22 RSV.

by the one man's disobedience the many were made sinners, so by the one man's obedience the many will be made righteous.....so that just as sin exercised dominion in death, so grace might also exercise dominion through justification leading to eternal life through Jesus Christ our Lord."[7]

In the Genesis story, God gave mankind dominion over the whole earth, "over every living thing that moves upon the earth."[8] Adam and Eve disobeyed God and were run out of the garden before they could eat fruit from the tree of life. They were thereby deprived of eternal life because of their disobedience. Mankind continued to attempt to live without God, somehow not choosing to comprehend and give glory to their Creator who had given them life and breath.

In the fullness of time when the Roman Empire had made travel and communication more feasible, Jesus came. He did not hold on to the privileges and riches of being like God. Instead he humbled himself and became a man of flesh like Adam. Jesus, however, was completely obedient to God even unto death. He fulfilled *God's plan* for mankind, described in Hebrews:

> *"What are human beings that you are mindful*
> *of them, or mortals, that you care for them? You*
> *have made them for a little while lower than the*
> *angels; you have crowned them with glory and*
> *honor, subjecting all things under their feet"*[9]

---

[7] Rom. 5:18,19,21 NRSV.

[8] Genesis 1:28b NRSV.

[9] Hebrews 2:6b-8a NRSV Adam Christology was apparently a common theme in early Christianity as attested to by the writer of Hebrews quoting from Psalm 8 and by the writings of Paul. For a fuller discussion see *The Theology of Paul the Apostle* by James Dunn, Grand Rapids, Mich., Wm. B.Eerdmans, 1998, pp 200-203.

Under the law, mankind could not fulfill this role because of sin. So Paul explains that God has done what mankind weakened by sin could not do. He sent his own Son in the likeness of Adam to take upon himself (who knew no sin) the sin of the world—to condemn that sin by his crucifixion.[10] Jesus agonized, suffered, and died for our sins; he died the death deserved by all sinners. But God raised him from the dead, breaking the power of death. He exalted him, putting him (under God the Father) over all creation and *extending his grace unto all who believe.*[11]

"We know that our old self was crucified with him so that the body of sin might be destroyed, and we might no longer be enslaved to sin."[12]

Jesus became the new perfect pattern for mankind, fulfilling all God's purposes for his creation. He thereby actually began a new people[13], who acknowledged their dependence upon God as Creator and *chose* to worship and obey him. The followers of Jesus were not born just through the flesh, but were reborn through faith in Him, receiving the Holy Spirit. Identifying with

---

[10] This must be accepted by faith, but for a foreshadowing of this sacrificial act of God see page 82.

[11] This whole passage is based on Romans 8, Galatians 4, 2 Corinthians 5 and Philippians 2.

[12] Romans 6: 6.

[13] Romans 8:29b NRSV. ",,,in order that he (Jesus) might be the firstborn within a large family." (My parentheses).

the life of Jesus, they died with him in baptism and rose with him to new life in the Holy Spirit. This led Paul to write, "Therefore if anyone is in Christ, he is a new *creation*; the old has passed away, behold the new has come."[14]

All history became known by this act of God in Jesus Christ. The calendar was divided by the time before Christ—BC and AD (in the year of our Lord). Most unfortunately, this *world view* of Paul's has been relegated by many to the past—even though by any measure it is infinitely superior to the various "isms" invented by mankind. Others in our society have never been given a real opportunity to understand this wonderful good news of God in Christ.

Today we again see the strong human tendency to live without God in our lives, *to worship the creature instead of the Creator*. There are persistent humanist movements to exclude God from all human activity—in schools and colleges, in public life, and in the area of human morality. Such movements are not what they claim to be—brave efforts to move freedom ahead with human values leading the way. They are in reality efforts to move backward into the morass which occasioned the original fall of mankind from grace.

As Paul said of the harassment of unbelieving Jews—"You have shown that you are not worthy of eternal life, I will go to the Gentiles." Today many do not seem to be interested in or perhaps worthy of eternal life. Let us, however, preach the word

---

[14] 2 Cor. 5:17 RSV.

of God to all who will listen, encouraging them with the good news of Christ.

13

Jerusalem
The End Of Paul's Freedom

The voyage to Jerusalem, ending the third missionary journey was filled with Holy Spirit warnings to Paul. At Tyre in Syria the brothers met with local disciples. Through the Spirit they sternly warned Paul not to go on to Jerusalem. It must have been a most difficult decision for Paul. The Spirit was warning him of disastrous consequences if he continued.

But Paul felt he had a special mission to accomplish. The collection from the predominantly Gentile churches had to be taken to the apostles and poor brothers. And Paul still was most concerned about his own people, the Jews, even as they plotted to kill him. When the ship reached Caesarea, Paul and his friends went into the house of Philip, the evangelist.

While staying there for several days, a prophet called Agabus[1] came from Jerusalem. He immediately took Paul's belt, lay down upon the floor, bound both his own hands and feet and proclaimed the following prophesy, "In this way the Jews in Jerusalem will bind the owner of this belt and hand him over to the Gentiles. Thus says the Holy Spirit." It was the most dramatic warning Paul had yet received.

Upon hearing this, all the disciples pleaded with Paul not to return to Jerusalem. But it was to no avail. Paul cried out, "Why are you weeping? You are breaking my heart; I am willing to face any danger, even death, in Jerusalem for the sake of the Lord." Realizing that he would not be persuaded, silence came upon them as they prayed for Paul's safety.

Criticism has been raised by some writers for Paul's continuing to Jerusalem in spite of the Spirit's warnings. They interpret Paul's action as disobedience and argue that Paul, had he heeded the Spirit's warnings, could have evangelized many other countries—even changed the course of human history.

But it was not just the giving of financial aid that was important. It was of equal importance for the Gentile Christians of Asia and Greece to respond to the saints who had given them such an abundance of spiritual assistance. Paul writes further, "So, when I have completed this, and have delivered to them what has been collected, I will set out by way of you (Rome) to

---

[1] Probably the same prophet who many years before had predicted the worldwide famine.

Spain, and I know that when I come to you, I will come in the fullness of the blessing of Christ."[2] Paul would go to Rome, but the warning of the Spirit would be fulfilled.

One of the mysteries of Acts is that nothing further is said about the collection, which had to be a substantial sum of money. After such a strenuous and sacrificial effort on Paul's part, it is certain that he delivered it to the apostles. Fulfilling its purpose, they undoubtedly distributed it to the poor Christians in Jerusalem. However, some of the Judaizers might have refused it on account of their deep distrust and enmity toward Paul. Acts is simply silent on the matter.

The believers in Jerusalem received Paul warmly and took him to see James and the other apostles, and he related all the things God had accomplished among the Gentiles through his ministry. They were very concerned about the unbelieving Jews and even the Judaizers, so they advised Paul to join four men, who were taking a vow. They also urged Paul to pay the cost of the other four. They felt this might satisfy the Judaizers and even some unbelieving Jews that Paul was indeed upholding his Jewish heritage.

This plan did not work, for when some Jews from Asia arrived, they stirred up the crowd, claiming that Paul had illegally taken Gentiles into the Temple. The charge was baseless, but it so infuriated the crowd, which was already wary of Paul, that they entered the temple, dragged Paul out and began beating him with their fists and feet.

As previously related, when the tribune arrived to quell the riot, Paul was put in chains and taken into the barracks. And

---

[2] Rom. 15:28, 29 NRSV (my parenthesis).

Paul addresses the mob in Jerusalem.

even though he was never really found guilty, he was to remain a prisoner for at least two years, primarily to please the traditional Jewish people. This state of affairs would have depressed most people and made it difficult for them to function at all, but even though age and punishments had slowed the once indomitable evangelist, his spirit was as strong as ever. He continued his evangelistic mission as a prisoner in chains.

Since the charges against Paul were fundamentally religious in nature, he was taken before the Sanhedrin to be judged. This "court" consisted almost totally of traditional Jews, all those who wanted to get rid of Paul. But Paul, knowing the marked difference between the Pharisees and the Sadducees over the resurrection of the dead, used the issue to turn the assembly into a turmoil. He was returned to the barracks with no verdict.

That night the Lord stood by Paul and said, "Keep up your courage. You have testified for me in Jerusalem, now you must testify for me in Rome."

14

Escape To Caesarea To Appear Before Felix

The young man was frightened and nervous. Lysias, the tribune, took his hand and drew him aside privately and in a calm voice said to him, "Son, do not be afraid. What have you to say to me?"

The boy, Paul's nephew, finally stammered, "The Jews have devised a plot to kill Paul. Forty of them have sworn an oath not to eat or drink 'til Paul is dead."

"How do they plan to carry this out?"

"They will ask you to take him before the council again tomorrow. The forty assassins will be lying in ambush."

"Tell no one that you have informed me," the tribune said in a hushed voice.. You may go now."

A centurion woke Paul up out of a comfortable sleep. His status as a Roman Citizen had saved him from being beaten. "Get up and dress quickly. We are sending you to Governor Felix in Caesarea." Paul was given a mount and was accompanied by two hundred soldiers, seventy horsemen and two hundred spearmen, enough to intimidate any number of assassins.

Lysias sent a note to Felix explaining the situation in regard to Paul. In the note, Lysias wrote, "I am sending him to Caesarea to prevent his assassination. I find that he was accused concerning questions of their law, but was charged with nothing deserving death or imprisonment."

Two days later Paul was presented to Felix along with the letter from Lysias.

"I will give you a hearing when your accusers arrive," the Governor pronounced. Then he ordered him to be kept under guard in Herod's headquarters.

Five days later the high priest, Ananias, arrived with a "stuffed-shirt" lawyer, named Tertullus. The trial was set and Tertullus began his speech with a multitude of flattering platitudes about Felix, finally accusing Paul of being a pestilent agitator wherever he went and of profaning the temple by bringing Gentiles there.

When Felix motioned for Paul to make his defense, the former prosecutor, made a brilliant speech, stating the truth—that he had come to bring an offering to the poor Christians in Jerusalem and had decided to take a vow. He was in the temple, undergoing his rite of purification without any crowd or disturbance when he was suddenly dragged out onto the street by an unruly mob. Before the council nothing had been proven of him by his accusers, and the reason he was now on trial was a question about the resurrection of the dead.

Felix, who was very well informed about the Way, dismissed the court and announced, "When Lysias, the tribune, comes down from Jerusalem, I will decide the case." He ordered Paul to be held in custody, but afforded him the liberty of seeing his friends.

Felix developed a keen curiosity in Paul's faith. He and his wife, Drusilla who was Jewish, sent for Paul and listened to the Gospel. But when Paul spoke of morality and the judgment, Felix became apprehensive and ended the conversation. Still, he sent for Paul several more times and engaged in serious conversation about the faith. However, being a political appointee of questionable character, Felix secretly hoped that Paul might offer him money.

Thus began a series of trials before different governors and even a king. Nothing damaging was ever proven against Paul, but the dignitaries, trying to please the Jews, kept Paul in prison for an indefinite period of time. His only contact with his churches would be by messenger or letter, and his fond hopes of ever evangelizing Spain seemed to be dashed. After two years had elapsed, Felix was replaced as governor by Porcius Festus.

15

A Political Prisoner Faces More Trials

The great hall was decorated with regal furnishings. Festus, the new Roman governor, entered with a flourish of trumpets and took his seat. With another sound of trumpets, King Agrippa and Bernice entered from the other end of the hall. Behind them in pecking order came the military tribunes, followed by the prominent men of the city. The King and Bernice marched to the elevated platform and took seats surrounding Festus. The other notables filed to each side of the hall. When all had taken their seats, Festus raised his hand and Paul, in chains, was brought in.

Festus began, "King Agrippa, noble lady and gentlemen, you see this man here before you. The whole Jewish community has petitioned me to put him to death, but I have found nothing deserving the death penalty. But when I suggested that he go up to Jerusalem and be tried before me, he appealed his case to his Imperial Majesty, the emperor. I decided to send him, but I had no real charges to put before the emperor. So I have brought him before all of you and especially King Agrippa for you to examine him, so that I might have specific charges to send to the emperor."

Agrippa then said to Paul, "You have permission to speak. Let us hear from you."

Paul, who had appealed to the emperor to avoid facing the assassins in Jerusalem, stretched out his hand and began his defense. "All the Jews know that I was raised according to the strict customs of our ancestors. They also know that I belonged to the strictest sect of our religion. I stand trial here today because of my hope in the promise God made to our ancestors, a promise that our twelve tribes hope to attain, as they earnestly worship each day. That hope is in the resurrection of the dead. Why do any of you think this hope is incredible?

"I myself was convinced that I should join the fight against Jesus of Nazareth. I was chosen by the chief priests and others in authority to prosecute the followers of the Way. This I did with great vigor, jailing many and putting other to death. By punishing them in all the synagogues, I hoped to force them to blaspheme. My relentless campaign against them even led me to foreign cities."

At this point Paul related in vivid detail his experience on the road to Damascus. He continued his defense by quoting the words Jesus had spoken to him: "I have appeared to you so that you can bear witness to the things you have seen and to the other times I will appear to you. I will deliver you from your people and from the Gentiles, to whom I send you—that they may turn from darkness to light, from Satan to God. That they might receive forgiveness of sins and be sanctified by faith in me.

"Therefore, King Agrippa, I was not disobedient to the heavenly vision. I made my witness first in Damascus, then in Jerusalem and throughout the country. I even went before the Gentiles so that they would repent and turn to God. For this reason the Jews seized me in the temple and tried to kill me. But I have had help from God, and I stand here before this great gathering, testifying about what the prophets said would come to pass—that the Messiah would have to suffer and rise from the dead—that he would bring salvation to both the Jews and the Gentiles."

At this point Festus exclaimed, "Paul, you are mad, your great learning is turning you mad."

"I am not mad, most excellent Festus. I am speaking most truthfully."

Paul then turned his attention to Agrippa. "The king knows about these things, for they were not done behind a curtain, so I will speak freely to you. King Agrippa, do you believe the prophets? I feel sure that you do."

Agrippa replied, *"Paul, you are almost persuading me to be a Christian."*

"I wish to God that I could with everyone here in this hall—that all of you might become as I am except for these chains."

101

Then the King, Bernice, and Festus rose and left the hall. Outside they confessed to one another, "This man surely does not deserve death or imprisonment."

And Agrippa said to Festus. "This man could have been freed, had he not appealed to the emperor."

Paul had been in prison more than two years because of the effort by two governors to appease the Jews. He had been backed into a corner by the threat of Festus to take him back to Jerusalem for trial. His plea to go before the emperor was granted, and he was now waiting for a ship to depart for Rome. His great wish to witness in Rome and join the believers there was about to be granted, but as a man in chains.

16

Desperate Adventure
At Sea

They set sail from Caesarea in an Adramyttium[1] ship, stopping at several ports along the coast of Asia. Paul was in the custody of a centurion of the Augustan Cohort[2] named Julius. The centurion liked Paul and granted him every possible privilege. The two men found that they had much in common. In the Roman Army Julius had fought bravely and suffered a

---

[1] A seaport east of Troas.

[2] In the Roman Army a cohort consisted of 6oo men. Each 100 men were under an officer called a centurion, who was picked for his character, loyalty and consistency. The Augustan Cohort, named after the emperor, was stationed at Caesarea during the early part of the 1st century.

Paul's Journey to Rome

Used by permission of Biblical Studies Press

104

number of wounds. His intelligence and loyalty had elevated him to the rank of centurion; and being assigned to special duty in Caesarea, he had come to respect Paul and was sympathetic to his plight.

The ship continued around the Mediterranean Coast past Cilicia and Pamphylia, putting in at the port of Myra. It was there that they boarded an Alexandrian ship bound for Italy. They sailed westward for several days against an unfavorable wind, turned south and sailed under the lee of Crete, putting into a port called Fair Havens.

Fall had come—a season of uncertain and sometimes dangerous sailing conditions. As they were waiting for the weather to turn, Paul spent much time in conversation with Julius discussing the Gospel. The centurion was very interested and asked many questions, but had not yet made an outward commitment.

When the wind turned favorable, barely producing a light chop on the placid blue water, the centurion and captain decided to put to sea; they both felt the need of a better harbor in which to winter. When Paul heard of their decision, he approached the two men and said, "Sirs, I believe it is too late in the year to risk further sailing. The voyage could definitely endanger the cargo, the ship and even our lives." Years of sailing the Mediterranean waters and even a shipwreck had given Paul a well seasoned knowledge of nautical conditions. But the centurion paid more attention to the captain, and so they set sail.

The ship had traveled only a few miles when the moderate south wind suddenly turned northeast, coming down from Crete. The blue sky and bright sunlight faded into a dull grey overcast. As the wind grew more violent, it became evident that the ship could not be turned into it to make another harbor in Crete. The only course was to drop the sails, let out the sea anchor and be driven by the wind. Coming under the lee of a small island, the crew was able to hoist the ship's boat onto the deck and undergird the ship with cables as a precaution against grounding.

The next day the storm grew much more violent and the pounding so severe that the captain ordered the crew to begin throwing cargo overboard. On the third day even the ship's tackle was cast overboard. The frightening waves reached over twenty feet in height with an occasional rogue wave drenching the entire deck. For many days, the sky was so black that no one could see the sun or stars.

The crew began to lose heart and consider that all hope of being saved was lost. A general malaise griped the whole ship. Paul then stood among them and said, "Men, you should have listened to me and avoided this fearful ordeal and loss. No one's life will be lost, only the ship, so keep up your courage. Last night an angel of the God I serve stood beside me and said, 'Do not fear, Paul, you must stand before Caesar. God has granted safety to all who sail with you.' I have faith in what God has told me. We must run the ship aground on some island."

On the fourteenth night as they were being driven across the sea, some of the sailors suspected the ship might be approaching land. They took a sounding and found twenty fathoms; a little further on they took another and found fifteen fathoms. Fearing that the ship might run aground on rocks, the captain ordered four anchors to be let down from the stern. They all waited, hoped, and prayed for daylight to come.

During this time several of the sailors, under the pretense of laying out anchors, attempted to lower the ship's boat, thinking they might escape in it. But Paul seeing their effort said to the centurion, "These men must stay on board if we are to be saved." The centurion immediately ordered the boat's ropes to be cut, losing it into the sea.

Then Paul said, "Men you have suffered much fear and tension for fourteen days during which time you have eaten little or nothing. You are going to need your strength, so I encourage you to take some food." He took bread and after giving thanks to God in the presence of all, he began to eat. The men (all two hundred and seventy six) much encouraged began to take some food.

In the morning an island became visible, and they saw a bay with a beach. The crew cast off the stern anchors and hoisted the foresail, making for the beach, but soon the ship ran aground on a reef. The stern, being pounded by the waves began to break up. Following the normal procedure, the soldiers wanted to kill the prisoners so that none could escape, but the centurion, in order to save Paul, kept them from carrying it out. He commanded those who could swim to jump into the sea and head for shore and the others to float ashore on boards and pieces broken off the ship. And so it was just as Paul had said: no one was lost

One by one and in small bunches the haggard and exhausted men washed up on the beach. They were met almost immediately by the natives, who showed them great kindness and sympathy. It had begun to turn cold and rain, so they built a large fire for the survivors, who all had a chance to warm themselves.

The haggard and exhausted men washed up on the beach.

Paul in his usual practical way was gathering wood. As he was putting it on the fire, a poisonous viper, driven out by the heat, struck Paul on the hand and fastened itself there. One of the natives cried out, "This man must be a murderer. Even though he escaped from the sea, justice will not allow him to live." The others nodded and whispered the same sentiment among themselves. Paul simply shook the snake off into the fire and went to gather more wood.

After he repeated this effort several times, the natives expected him to swell up and die, but a long time ensued and Paul showed no effects from the bite. Then a new sentiment passed through the crowd. Again they said to each other, "We have never seen a person survive that viper. This man must be a god." Understanding their change of mind, Paul could not help recalling the reverse experience that happened in Lystra, when in a matter of minutes he was called a god by the crowd and then stoned by a raging mob.

The leading man of the island called Malta was named Publius. His lands were near the beach where the survivors had washed ashore. He received all the cast-a-ways with kindness and fed and entertained them for several days. The father of Publius was sick in bed, and when Paul found out, he went, laid hands on him and prayed for him. When the father recovered, the people of the island brought all their sick to Paul who healed them. They bestowed many honors on Paul and his companions and gave them provisions to take onboard the ship when they sailed.

Three months later, Paul and his friends together with Julius, the centurion, and a few others boarded an Alexandrian ship, which had wintered at the island. They had favorable weather and stopped for a short time in Syracuse on the island of Sicily and then in Rhegium, on the toe of the Italian boot.

A fresh south wind sprang up, so they made good time, arriving at Puteoli, a seaport only a short distance from Rome. Paul and his friends were welcomed there by a group of believers, who invited them to stay for seven days. Afterwards, they left for Rome and were met by Roman Christians, who had come as far as the Forum of Appius to greet them. Paul, on seeing them, thanked God and took heart.

17

In Rome, A Minister In Chains, Circa 61-63 A.D.

From the account in Acts, Paul's next two years in Rome were quite productive. He was allowed to stay at his own dwelling with a soldier guarding him at all times. As he had done so many times on his journeys, he first called the leaders of the Roman Jews together. He then related the events which had brought him to Rome in chains. After hearing from Paul, they said to him, "We have received no letters from Judea about you, neither have any of the brethren arriving here spoken anything evil about you. The sect to which you belong has received much bad testimony, but we would like to hear more from you." So a day was appointed, and large numbers of Jews came to Paul's lodging.

With his usual energy and skill, Paul expounded the Gospel to them from morning till evening, trying to convince them that Jesus was the Messiah spoken of by the prophets, the psalms, and by Moses. Some of the Jews believed, while others were not persuaded and so they argued among themselves, causing Paul to quote Isaiah the prophet who spoke the words of the Holy Spirit:

> *"You shall indeed hear but never understand, and you shall indeed see, but never perceive, For the people's heart has grown dull, and their ears are heavy of hearing, and their eyes they have closed..."*[1]

Paul then pronounced, "I will take the word of God for salvation to the Gentiles. They will listen."

For two years Paul was allowed to teach the Gospel to all who would come and listen. A great many did come and so, even as a prisoner, Paul's work was unhindered. During this period Paul also wrote letters to Philemon, the Colossians, Ephesians and Philippians while still being guarded by a Roman soldier. He even indicates in Philippians that his imprisonment helped to spread the Gospel even to the whole imperial guard. It was a productive time for the word of God with Paul continuing to show his great spirit and determination.

Following these two years, there is no authentic record of Paul, which leaves scholars and biographers room to speculate and wonder. It is quite possible he appeared before the emperor.

---

[1] Isaiah 6:9b, 10a NRSV.

Some think Paul never received his freedom, while others believe that he was set free to resume his journeys for another two years.

Some even think that he did make it to Spain and returned to several of his churches. This latter concept of Paul's story is not only intriguing, it is supported by the fact that no real case against him was sent to Rome. Also it is hardly likely that a prisoner on "death row" would have been accorded such extraordinary privileges. One thing is certain: he never gave up; his spirit never became dull, and he never stopped teaching the Gospel and proclaiming Christ.

The great fire in Rome for which Christians were unjustly blamed occurred in 64 AD. The result was a severe persecution against all Christians and especially against their leaders. Paul most likely was arrested in Asia Minor and brought to Rome where many speculate that Nero or his cohorts sentenced Paul to death. Being a Roman citizen, his sentence was a quick and less painful death—beheading. He probably spent some time in a dark and cramped Roman prison before being marched outside the walls of Rome by a detachment of soldiers and beheaded. The year was around 66 AD.

Earlier he had written to the Philippians, "Yes, and I shall rejoice. For I know that through your prayers and the help of the Spirit of Jesus Christ this will turn out for my deliverance, as it is my eager expectation and hope that I shall not be at all ashamed, but with full courage now as always Christ will he honored in my body, whether by life or by death. For to me to live is Christ, and to die is gain. If it is to be life in the flesh, that means fruitful labor for me. Yet which I shall choose I cannot tell. I am hard pressed between the two. My desire is to depart and be with Christ, for that is far better."(Phil.1:19-23 RSV).

And in 2nd Timothy Paul wrote these last poignant words, "For I am already on the point of being sacrificed; the time of my departure has come. I have fought the good fight, I have finished the race. I have kept the faith. Henceforth there is laid up for me the crown of righteousness, which the Lord, the righteous judge, will award to me on that Day, and not only to me but also to all who have loved his appearing."[2]

The last feeling in Paul's heart was great joy for he knew that at the stroke of the sword, he would at last be in the company of his beloved Savior.

Today, the beautiful Basilica of St. Paul outside the Walls stands over the place believed to be St. Paul's burial. It is not far from the Ostian Way, the scene of his execution. In 2002 and 2003 a sarcophagus was discovered under the main altar of the Basilica. It was located beneath a thick marble slab containing the following words:

PAULO APOSTOLO MART[3]

Death is a subject Paul had to deal with often in his letters. Early in his ministry the Thessalonians had written asking about

---

[2] 2nd Timothy 4:6-8 RSV.
[3] Translated "Apostle Paul, Martyr."

the fate of those who had died before the return of Christ. Paul writes that those who are alive at the Parousia (return of Christ) will not precede those who have died. When the Lord descends from heaven, the dead in Christ will rise first. At this time Paul, like many others, felt that the coming of Christ would occur in his lifetime. As his ministry progressed through many years, Paul's thoughts began to change.

1st Corinthians 15 contains a long essay about death and resurrection. Apparently, in answer to a question posed by the Corinthians, Paul writes words to this effect: "If Christ is proclaimed to be raised from the dead, how can some of you say there is no resurrection of the dead? If there is no resurrection, then Christ has not been raised and our proclamation of the good news is in vain. Then those who have died in Christ have perished. If it is only in this life that we have hoped in Christ, we are of all people most to be pitied.

"But in fact Christ has been raised, the first fruits of those who have died. For since by one man death came into the world, so also the resurrection of the dead has come by another man, Jesus Christ. But each must come in his own order. At the coming of Christ, those who are his own will be raised." Paul is still thinking of the resurrection of the dead occurring at the time of Christ's second coming.

Paul also answers a question about what kind of body those raised will have. He compares the dying body to something else in nature—a bare seed, which he explains is sown into the ground. The seed dies, but God gives it a new body as he chooses. As our bodies die in Christ, God gives us a new body, a spiritual body like Christ's body at the resurrection. For flesh and blood cannot inherit the kingdom of God, only spiritual bodies can. And he thanks God who gives us this victory through our Lord Jesus Christ.

A full statement of this transformation is found in Philippians. "But our citizenship is in heaven, and it is from there that we are expecting a Savior, the Lord Jesus Christ. He will transform the body of our humiliation that it may be conformed to the body of his glory, by the power that also enables him to make all things subject to himself."[4]

In 2nd Corinthians Paul makes a remarkable statement about growing older and suffering various ailments. He exhorts us not to lose heart. For, he writes, *"Even though our outer nature is wasting away, our inner nature is being renewed day by day."* For this slight momentary affliction is preparing us for an eternal weight of glory beyond all measure...For we know that if the earthly tent we live in is destroyed, we have a building from God, a house not made with hands, eternal in the heavens. For in this tent we groan, longing to be clothed with our heavenly dwelling...For while we are still in this tent, we groan under our burden, because we wish not to be unclothed but to be further clothed, so that what is mortal may be swallowed up by life. He who has prepared us for this very thing is *God, who has given us the Spirit as a guarantee."*[5]

In Romans there is a further elaboration on this approach: "If the Spirit of him who raised Jesus from the dead dwells in you, he who raised Christ from the dead will give life to your mortal bodies also through his Spirit who dwells in you."[6] *There is no mention of a period of time between death and resurrection*

---

[4] Phil. 3:20, 21 NRSV.
[5] 2nd Corinthians 4:16b-5:5 NRSV (my italics).
[6] Romans 8:11 NRSV.

occurring at the Parousia. The chapter ends with the great and familiar passage by Paul:

"For I am convinced that neither death, nor life, nor angels, nor rulers, nor things present nor things to come, nor powers, nor height, nor depth, nor anything else in all creation, will be able to separate us from the love of God in Christ Jesus our Lord."[7]

And repeating the Philippians phrase discussing life and death, "I am hard pressed between the two; my desire is to *depart and to be with Christ,* for that is far better…"[8]

Paul finishes his discussion of death in 1st Corinthians with this remarkable warning and consolation: "The sting of death is sin, and the power of sin is the law. *But thanks be to God, who gives us the victory through our Lord Jesus Christ.* Therefore, my beloved, be steadfast, immovable, always excelling in the work of the Lord, because you know that in the Lord your labor is not in vain."[9]

As Paul's thinking matured concerning the resurrection of the dead, he began to understand that the Parousia might not take place during his lifetime. He was firm in his belief that the same Spirit who raised Jesus would also raise Christians—if the Spirit was indeed present in them. And he believed that the resurrection body would be like that of Christ's. But the delay of the Parousia would not delay the resurrection of the dead. By the time he wrote Philippians, he was certain that to die would mean being immediately in the presence of Christ for all Spirit-filled Christians.

---

[7] Romans 8:38,39 NRSV.
[8] Phil.1:23 NRSV (my italics).
[9] 1st Corinthians 15:56,58 NRSV (my italics).

Part Three

Further Reflections On Paul's Character And Theology

18

Other Characteristics Of Paul

Paul was indeed an apostle, but he was also a pastor to all his churches, and his letters compose a theology still considered foremost in the church. But was Paul a mystic, a person who is privileged to see and understand things no ordinary human can experience? His common sense, commitment, and determination do not come down hard on that side, but his experiences with the Lord and his visions indicate otherwise.

Principal among these was his experiencing the Lord on the Damascus road. Regardless of how many times Paul describes this scene, none do it justice, for it turned the most passionate opponent of Jesus into his most zealous servant. And this was not for a short time, it was for a whole lifetime of hardship, suffering, and strife—driven by a conviction and determination seldom seen in any man. This fact alone should convince the most skeptical of its absolute authenticity.

But this was only the beginning. Christ appeared to him in visions while he was in the Arabian Desert. In Corinth in a vision the Lord spoke to Paul, assuring him and telling him, "I have many people in this city." The Lord also came and stood by his side when he was in chains in Jerusalem, giving him great encouragement. On the second missionary journey Paul in a vision saw a man in Macedonia pleading for the evangelists to come and help them. During the fearful shipwreck, an angel of the Lord stood by Paul one night, telling him to take heart—that God had granted safety to all those sailing with him—that the lives of everyone on board would be spared. These are just some of the mystical experiences described in Acts.

Paul's most unusual mystical experience is recorded in 2nd Corinthians. The apostle was again defending himself against the purveyors of a false gospel: "…I will go on to visions and revelations of the Lord. I know a person in Christ who fourteen years ago was caught up to the third heaven—whether in the body or out of the body I do not know; God knows—was caught up into Paradise and heard things that are not to be told, that no mortal is permitted to repeat. On behalf of such a one I will boast, but on my own behalf I will not boast, except of my weaknesses. But if I wish to boast, I will not be a fool, for I will be speaking the truth. But I refrain from it, so that no one will think better of me than what is seen in me or heard from me,

even considering the exceptional character of the revelations."[1]
There is no doubt that Paul was speaking about himself.

A characteristic of Paul which is sometimes overlooked is his emphasis on love. This at times is obscured by his extensive parenthesis or exhortation against the moral laxity of his day. However, this aspect of his personality should not be surprising since Paul followed Jesus in this regard.

Paul loved the people of his congregations. This is evident in all his letters. To the Philippians he wrote, " Therefore my brothers and sisters, whom I *love* and long for, my joy and crown, stand firm in the Lord…" He almost apologizes if he has to correct them, and in most of his letters he takes great pains to recognize those who are faithful and are doing great work in Christ.

In Romans, Paul wrote, "The commandments are summed up in this statement, "You shall *love* your neighbor as yourself. *Love* does no wrong to a neighbor; therefore *love* is the fulfilling of the law."[2]

And conversely, "Bless those who curse you; bless and do not curse them….No, if your enemy is hungry, feed him; if he is thirsty, give him drink; for by so doing you will heap burning coals upon his head. Do not be overcome by evil, but overcome evil with good."[3]

He wrote to the Galatians, "For the whole law is fulfilled in

---

[1] 2nd Cor. 12:1b-7a NRSV.
[2] Rom. 13:9b,10 RSV.
[3] Rom. 12:14,20,21 RSV, also a reiteration of Prov. 25:21,22.

one word. You shall *love* your neighbor as yourself."[4]

In Paul's letter to the Ephesians we find, "…and that Christ may dwell in your hearts through faith; that you being rooted and grounded in *love*, may have power to comprehend with all the saints what is the breadth and length and height and depth, and to know the *love* of Christ which surpasses knowledge, that you may be filled with all the fullness of God."[5]

And then there is Paul's crowning discourse on love in 1st Corinthians 13. Paul writes, "*Love* is patient and kind, *love* is not jealous or boastful; it is not arrogant or rude. *Love* does not insist on its own way; it is not irritable or resentful; it does not rejoice at wrong, but rejoices in the right. *Love* bears all things, believes all things, hopes all things, endures all things. *Love* never ends…. So faith, hope, *love* abide, these three, but the greatest of these is *love*."[6] May we all have the great blessing of giving and receiving such love as this.

---

[4] Galatians 5:14 RSV.
[5] Ephesians 3:17-19 RSV.
[6] 1 Cor. 13:4-8a,13 RSV.

19

The Prayer Life Of St. Paul

When we think of St. Paul, the immediate picture which comes to mind is a hard driving, resilient person who is always moving forward with unmatched energy and determination. And while this description is part of his personality, there is much more. After his encounter with Christ on the road to Damascus, Ananias finds Paul, a blind and helpless man, praying. Paul was praying in the temple when the Lord appeared to him and warned him to leave Jerusalem.[1]

---

[1] Based on Acts 22:17,18.

On the second missionary journey when Paul and Silas were locked up in jail in Philippi, they began praying and singing hymns to God before the earthquake took place. And when Paul bade farewell to the elders of Ephesus, he knelt down and prayed with them all.

On Malta when visiting the sick father of Publius, Paul prayed with him before putting his hands upon him and healing him. And so we see that Paul was certainly a man of prayer, who depended upon the Lord's direction before making important decisions.

In his letters we find some of Paul's prayers. They are basically addressed to the churches, but they nevertheless reflect the prayers of Paul. To the Ephesians Paul writes, "For this reason I bow my knees before the Father, from whom every family in heaven and on earth is named, that according to the riches of his glory he may grant you to be strengthened with might through his Spirit in the inner man, and that Christ may dwell in your hearts through faith....Now to him who by the power at work within us is able to do far more abundantly than all that we ask or think, to him be glory in the church and in Christ Jesus to all generations, for ever and ever. Amen."[2]

Also in Ephesians Paul states, "I do not cease to give thanks for you, remembering you in my prayers, that the God of our Lord Jesus Christ, the Father of glory, may give you a spirit of wisdom and revelation in the knowledge of him, having the eyes of your hearts enlightened, that you may know what is the

---

[2] Eph. 3:14-17a, 20, 21 RSV.

hope to which he has called you, what are the riches of his glorious inheritance in the saints…"[3]

In Philippians Paul writes, "I thank my God in all my remembrance of you, always in every prayer of mine for you all making my prayer with joy, thankful for your partnership in the gospel from the first day until now. . . . And it is my prayer that your love may abound more and more, with knowledge and all discernment, so that you may approve what is excellent, and may be pure and blameless for the day of Christ , filled with the fruits of righteousness which come through Jesus Christ, to the glory and praise of God."[4]

Paul writes to the Colossians, "And so from the day we heard of it (your love in the Spirit), we have not ceased to pray for you, asking that you may be filled with the knowledge of his will in all spiritual wisdom and understanding, to lead a life worthy of the Lord, fully pleasing to him, bearing fruit in every good work and increasing in the knowledge of God."[5]

Paul's prayer for the Thessalonians was, "To this end we always pray for you, that our God may make you worthy of his call, and may fulfill every good resolve and work of faith by his power, so that the name of our Lord Jesus may be glorified in you, and you in him, according to the grace of our God and the Lord Jesus Christ."[6]

At the end of the letter to the Romans Paul writes, "Now to him who is able to strengthen you according to my gospel and the preaching of Jesus Christ, according to the revelation of the

---

[3] Eph. 1:16-18 RSV.
[4] Phil. 1:3-5, 9-11 RSV.
[5] Col. 1:9, 10 RSV. (My parenthesis)
[6] Thes. 1:11, 12 RSV.

mystery which was kept secret for long ages but is now disclosed and through the prophetic writings is made known to all nations, according to the command of the eternal God, to bring about obedience to the faith—to the only wise God be glory for evermore through Jesus Christ! Amen."[7]

These passages are indicative of the way Paul continuously prayed, especially for the churches he established. More than anything else, they show his dependence on God and a constant attitude of prayer and petition for the new churches—holding them up to God for their spiritual strengthening.

---

[7] Rom. 16:25-27 RSV.

20

On Christian Marriage

Paul generally follows the instructions of Jesus concerning marriage: it is between a man and a woman, and they are to become one flesh. If a man divorces his wife and marries another woman, he commits adultery against her. If the wife divorces her husband and marries another man, she commits adultery.[1]

Paul enlarges on these principles in Corinthians, chapter seven. He gives advice about marrying or not marrying based upon his understanding that Christ will return in the near future.

---

[1] Mark 10:6-12.

129

What is more important for us today is his advice to a Christian man or woman who marries an unbeliever. They should not divorce since an unbelieving husband can be made holy through his believing wife and visa versa, and he ends this exhortation by writing that the believing partner might very well save the unbeliever. There certainly are examples of this scenario in today's society where the believing partner by patience, prayer, and example ends up saving the other partner.

The Apostle, however, brings in his pattern of authority, which as mentioned before, derives from Hebrew scripture: "But I want you to understand that Christ is the head of every man, and the husband is the head of his wife, and God is the head of Christ."[2] And even though Paul holds to this order, he always brings in a little balance. For, a few sentences later he declares, "Nevertheless in the Lord woman is not independent of man or man independent of woman. For just as woman came from man, so man comes through woman, but all things come from God."[3]

It is evident in Ephesians that Paul follows this same order of authority in relation to marriage. He writes that wives are to be subject to their husbands as they are to the Lord. He then cites his authority for such a statement by writing that the husband is head of the wife just as Christ is head of the church, and that as the church is subject to Christ, wives should be subject to their husbands. This is the passage which inflames feminists in today's society. Again, Paul is not nearly through with this subject.

---

[2] 1st Cor. 11:3, 4 NRSV.
[3] 1st Cor. 11:11, 12 NRSV.

Paul sticks to his natural order. However, he evens the score in the passages which follow. "Husbands, love your wives, just as Christ loved the church and gave himself up for her, in order to make her holy by cleansing her…so that she may be made holy and without blemish. In the same way, husbands should love their wives as they do their own bodies. He who loves his wife loves himself. For no one ever hates his own body, but he nourishes and tenderly cares for it, just as Christ does for the church…Each of you, however, should love his wife as himself, and a wife should respect her husband."[4]

Our society is not anywhere near perfect or even somewhat successful when it comes to marriage. The divorce rate remains very high, and in many marriages there is little respect from either side, with some marriages ending in excessive violence. Perhaps, more serious thought should be given to the Apostle's words, which might put marriage on a sounder and more successful basis.

---

[4] Eph. 5:25-33 NRSV.

21

Exhortations Of Paul

At the end of several of Paul's letters, he gives the new churches very practical advice. This advice is as timely to us today as it was to the churches 2000 years ago. He advises the Galatians not to use their freedom to practice self-indulgence, but to use it by demonstrating love to one another.

He states again that what the flesh desires is opposed to the Spirit, and he lists the works of the flesh including fornication, licentiousness, idolatry, strife, jealousy, anger, quarrels, and carousing. In contrast, he lists the fruit of the Spirit which include love, joy, peace, patience, gentleness, and self-control. He reminds the Galatians that they will reap what they sow. If they sow to the flesh, they will reap corruption, but if they sow to the Spirit they will reap eternal life.

In Ephesians Paul admonishes children to obey their parents, telling them that this is the first commandment which promises a reward—long life on the earth. Conversely, he tells fathers not to provoke their children to anger, but to teach them discipline and the word of the Lord.

In Colossians Paul writes: "bearing with one another, and forgiving each other... just as the Lord forgave you, so also should you. Beyond all these things *put on* love, which is the perfect bond of unity. Let the peace of Christ rule in your hearts, to which indeed you were called in one body; and be thankful. Let the word of Christ richly dwell within you, with all wisdom teaching and admonishing one another with psalms *and* hymns *and* spiritual songs, singing with thankfulness in your hearts to God. Whatever you do in word or deed, do all in the name of the Lord Jesus, giving thanks through Him to God the Father."[1]

Paul counsels, "Do not lag in zeal, be ardent in spirit, serve the Lord. Rejoice in hope, be patient in suffering, persevere in prayer. Contribute to the needs of the saints; extend hospitality to strangers."[2]

In the last chapter of Philippians Paul writes a beautiful and familiar passage: "Rejoice in the Lord always; again I will say, Rejoice.... Have no anxiety about anything, but in everything by prayer and supplication with thanksgiving let your requests be made known to God. And the peace of God, which passes all

---

[1] Col. 3:13-17 NASB.

[2] Rom. 12:11-13 NRSV.

understanding, will keep your hearts and your minds in Christ Jesus."[3]

"We ask you, brothers, to respect those who labor among you and are over you in the Lord and admonish you, and to esteem them very highly in love because of their work,"[4] Paul wrote in the first letter to the Thessalonians.

Everyone who reads Acts or Paul's letters knows that he was never idle. He worked with his hands weaving tents, sails, and coverings. This ethic comes out clearly at the end of 2nd Thessalonians where he writes that he hears that some are living in idleness, not doing any work. "For even when we were with you, we gave you this command: If any one will not work, let him not eat."[5] And in a number of letters Paul advises correcting a brother or sister in a spirit of gentleness—never in a spirit of anger.

"Finally, brethren, whatever is true, whatever is honorable, whatever is just, whatever is pure whatever is lovely, whatever is gracious, if there is any excellence, if there is anything worthy of praise, think about there things…and the God of peace will be with you."[6]

---

[3] Phil. 4:4-7 RSV

[4] 1 Thes. 5:12, 13

[5] 2nd Thes. 3:10 RSV

[6] Phil. 4:8,9 RSV

22

The Question Of Predestination and Israel

One of the most important chapters in Paul's letters is Romans 8. In the midst of this chapter we find a paragraph which gives the impression that Paul has an all-encompassing theology of predestination. The paragraph in question reads, "We know that all things work together for good for those who love the God, who are called according to his purpose. For those whom he foreknew he also predestined to be conformed to the image of his Son, in order that he might be the firstborn within a large family. And those whom he predestined he also called…"[1]

Such a view is hardly acceptable as can be clearly seen as we read on in chapters 9-11, which deal primarily with the question of Israel. Paul is so anguished about his own people, the Jews, that he makes the statement that he is willing to be accursed and cut off from Christ for the sake of his own kindred. They are the Israelites, whom God chose to be his people and gave them the covenants, the law, and the patriarchs.

By using the Hebrew scripture Paul shows how God chose some patriarchs of Israel even before they were born. An example would be the choosing of Jacob over his brother Esau even though Esau was born first. This choice was made before the boys were born as their mother, Rebecca, was told the older would serve the younger. Paul concludes that it depends on God's choice, not upon human will or exertion.

On the other hand, Paul goes on to quote from Hosea, who prophesied that "those who were not my people I will call 'my people,'… "[2] And he quotes Isaiah concerning Israel proclaiming, "Though the number of the children of Israel were like the sand of the sea, only a remnant of them will be saved…"[3] Paul is moving away from the all encompassing position of predestination as it pertains to Israel.

Why did the larger part of the Jews who strived for righteousness fail? They tried to do it on the basis of works not

---

[1] Rom. 8:28, 29, 30a NRSV.
[2] Rom. 9:25 NRSV.
[3] Rom. 9:27b NRSV.

on the basis of faith, and they stumbled over the stumbling stone. Paul then quotes Isaiah:

> *"See, I am laying in Zion a stone that will make people stumble, a rock that will make them fall, and whoever believes in him will not be put to shame."*[4]

Paul states that in seeking to establish their own righteousness, the Jews did not submit to God's righteousness. "For Christ is the end of the law so that *there may be righteousness for everyone who believes.*"[5]

Let anyone who is confused about predestination in regard to Paul read the following definitive statement from Romans: "…if you confess with your lips that Jesus is Lord and believe in your hearts that God raised him from the dead, you will be saved. For one believes from the heart and so is justified, and one confesses with the mouth and so is saved. The scripture says, 'No one who believes in him will be put to shame.' For there is no distinction between Jew and Greek, the same Lord is Lord of all and is generous to all who call on him. For, 'Everyone who calls on the name of the Lord will be saved.' "[6]

The preceding statements clearly show that the stumbling stone in Zion is Jesus and that all who have faith in him will be saved. According to Paul, God in the new covenant provides justification by faith as the way to salvation. And in Acts, we recall the simple question the jailor at Philippi addressed to Paul and Silas, "Sirs, what must I do to be saved?"

---

[4] Rom. 9:33 NRSV. Also refers back to Isaiah 28:16 and 8:14.
[5] Rom. 10:4 NRSV (my italics).
[6] Rom. 10: 9b-13 NRSV.

They answered, "Believe on the Lord Jesus and you will be saved."[7]

But what will happen to the Jews, historic Israel? In Romans, chapter 11, Paul pictures faithful Israel as a cultivated olive tree. God has broken the unbelieving branches off so that believing branches of a wild olive tree (Gentiles) might be grafted in. The true *Israel* then is not the nation or the race, but consists of all those who accept and believe in Christ. The roots of the cultivated olive tree, consisting of the promise, the patriarchs, and covenants, continue to provide nourishment.

Paul argues that the hardening of the unbelieving Jew's hearts was necessary in order for the Gospel to be spread to the world (Gentiles). Otherwise the Gospel might have remained only a Jewish faith. The entrance of the believing Gentiles has made the Jews jealous because of the Gentiles' many blessings. And when the full number of Gentiles has come in, all Israel will be saved[8]. "As regards the gospel, they (the Jews) are enemies of God for your (Gentiles) sake, but regards election (or predestination) they are beloved, for the sake of their ancestors; for the gifts and the calling of God are irrevocable."[9]

---

[7] Acts 16:30b,31a NRSV.

[8] There are two theories about "all Israel." One states that "all Israel" refers to a believing remnant who later become a majority. Supporting this theory is Paul's statement in Rom.11:23, which reads, "And even those of Israel, *if they do not persist in unbelief,* will be grafted in…" The other states that "all Israel" means just what it says—that all Israel will be saved by election, no exceptions.

[9] Rom. 11:28, 29 NRSV (my parenthesis).

23

The Crucifixion of Jesus As A Reflection of The Jewish Sacrificial Rite

In Paul's Gospel message there is a thread of interpreting the crucifixion of Jesus in terms of the Jewish sacrificial rite. In the sin offering, the sinner brought an animal without blemish to be sacrificed. The sinner's hands were placed upon the animal's head thereby transferring the sins to the animal, which was sacrificed in place of the sinner. On the day of Atonement the sins of the nation were confessed over a goat, which was led outside the camp into the wilderness. The sins of the people were thereby taken away (for that year until the next year when the same sacrifice was made again).

In a manner similar to the sacrificial rite, Jesus, who had led a perfect life, took upon himself all the transgressions of humanity. John the Baptist in the Gospel of John says, "Behold, the lamb of God who takes away the sin of the world." These sins were nailed to the cross with Jesus, and when he died these sins were condemned, erased, and abolished. In this sense Jesus died in place of sinners, as in the sacrificial rite where the perfect animal died in place of the sinful person or persons.

One other comparison with a significant Jewish experience is the Passover. At that time in Egypt, a lamb's blood was smeared on each Jewish doorpost to ward off the angel of death. In this way, Jesus is figuratively the slain lamb whose blood wards off death. Thus Jesus is our Passover lamb or rather our passover from death to life

According to Paul, however, there are several essential differences. Jesus took upon himself the sins of all humanity for all time. Therefore the sins of all who believe in Jesus, identify with him, and receive him as Master and Savior have been forgiven and continue to be forgiven as believers confess and repent—his righteousness being transferred continually to repentant sinners. The writer of Hebrews states that the perfect sacrifice of Jesus, offered for the sins of all people is sufficient for all time and no further sacrifices are needed (Hebrews, chapter 10).

In the crucifixion of Jesus *the sacrifice was furnished by God, himself.* Paul wrote in Romans, " He who did not withhold his own Son, but gave him up for all of us..."[1]

And again in Romans, "...since all have sinned and fall short of the glory of God, they are justified by his grace as a gift, through the redemption which is in Christ Jesus, *whom God put forward as an expiation by his blood, to be received by faith.* This was to show God's righteousness, because in his divine forbearance he has passed over former sins; it was to prove at the present time that he himself is righteous and that he justifies him who has faith in Jesus."[2]

The final great difference is that Jesus was raised from the dead to become the central figure in the salvation process. This is a recurring theme in Paul's letters.

---

[1] Rom. 8:32 This verse is reminiscent of Abraham's willingness to sacrifice his only son (the Aqedah). God provided a ram as substitute for Isaac.

[2] Rom. 3:23-26 RSV.

24

Not By Ourselves Alone

Life is meant to be lived in relationship with God, our Creator. Paul clearly defines this principle by the expression "in Christ," which occurs dozens of times in his letters. The other aspect of this same principle is the constant presence of the Holy Spirit after a person has accepted Christ.

In Ephesians Paul addressing the Gentiles writes, "remember that you were at that time without Christ, being aliens from the commonwealth of Israel, and strangers to the covenants of promise, having no hope and without God in the world. But now *in Christ Jesus* you who once were far off have been brought near by the blood of Christ."[1] "Having no hope and without God in the world," is a fearsome and terribly ill boding phrase. In fact, it speaks of sin and death as the two most compelling factors in the human drama.

When Adam and Eve disobeyed God and essentially broke off their relationship with him, they tried to hide from him. God made this frightening pronouncement, "By the sweat of your face you shall eat bread until you return to the ground, for out of it you were taken; you are dust and to dust you shall return." They were banished from the garden and never allowed to eat of the tree of life. In the following ages we know that mankind tried to live without God many times. Futility and a sense of discomposure were the inevitable results.

On the other hand, Paul asserts in Romans, "For the law of the Spirit of life *in Christ Jesus* has set you free from the law of sin and of death."[2] Again in Romans, "You must consider yourselves dead to sin and alive to God *in Christ Jesus*.[3] Also in 2nd Corinthians Paul writes, "Therefore if any one is *in Christ*, he is a new creation; the old has passed away, behold, the new has come....God was in Christ reconciling the world to himself, not counting their trespasses against them... For our sake he made him to be sin who knew no sin, so that in him we might become the righteousness of God."[4] And in Romans, "...the free gift of God is eternal life *in Christ Jesus* our Lord."[5] There are in these phrases a strong sense of participation in the new

---

[1] Eph. 2:12, 13 NRSV (my italics).
[2] Rom. 8:2 NRSV.
[3] Rom. 6:11 RSV.
[4] 2nd Corinthians 5:17, 19a, 21 RSV.
[5] Rom. 6:23b NRSV.

creation effected through Christ and a promise of individual salvation through faith in Him—*in Christ.*

> *After the last supper Jesus addressed his disciples, "If you love me, you will keep my commandments. And I will pray the Father, and he will give you another Counselor, to be with you for ever, even the Spirit of truth, whom the world cannot receive, because it neither sees him nor knows him; you know him, for he dwells with you, and will be in you."[6] (He said this fulfilling the prophecy of Joel who, speaking the words of the Lord, proclaimed, "And it shall come to pass afterward, that I will pour out my spirit on all flesh.)"[7]*

Paul declares to the Corinthians, "Or do you not know that your body is a temple of the Holy Spirit who is in you, whom you have from God…?[8] To Paul the Spirit was the discerning mark of every person who had heard the Gospel and believed in Christ. The Spirit was an experienced reality for Christian life from beginning to end.

How is the Spirit manifested in Christians? He keeps us always mindful of Jesus Christ. He energizes us and shows us the truth. According to Paul, the Spirit shapes our personalities to show forth love, joy, peace, patience, kindness, goodness, faithfulness, gentleness and self-control;[9] he imparts to us gifts

---

[6] John 14:15-17 RSV (my italics).

[7] Joel 2:28a RSV.

[8] 1st Cor. 6:19a NASB.

[9] The Holy Spirit enables Christians to show forth these qualities continually every day, in every situation, and to every person encountered.

such as prophecy, teaching, administration, and many others which build up the church. He teaches us how to pray. Paul further states that the Spirit is our guarantor of eternal life.

Today, when we are tempted to listen to *another gospel*, Paul would say that the Spirit intervenes and leads us back to the truth, the real Gospel of Jesus Christ, crucified for our sins and resurrected for our eternal salvation. And so we live in a constant relationship with the Creator *in Jesus Christ* and with the ever present Holy Spirit. How could we be more blessed?

Epilogue

Paul had to fight against every culture he addressed. In Israel, his own people, the unbelieving Jews, were incensed at his teaching; they declared him public enemy number one. At every turn they tried to kill him in order to silence his persuasive and intellectual Christian voice. They continually used their influence with the Romans to have him kept in chains to stop his amazing evangelistic success.

In pagan cultures which included all Gentile nations, Paul introduced a new religion which denied the power of all pagan gods and eventually led to their demise. His work in Ephesus enraged the artisans who produced silver shrines of Artemis. In Lystra the people tried to turn Paul and Barnabas into pagan gods, but Paul declared their belief in those gods to be futile and worthless. Moments later they stoned Paul.

To a certain extent in Israel and in all pagan countries like Greece, women were treated as mere possessions rather than marriage partners or equal members of the family. The father and the husband exercised dictatorial power over women. They had no real rights. Paul, although influenced by Hebrew scripture, nevertheless gave women a greater voice and value.

In addition, Paul, unlike the Jews, gave women a much greater role in the church. They were not divided from the men during the service, and some held important positions such as deacons.

In issues of morality, particularly sexual morality, forgiveness, and treatment of one's enemies, Paul's teaching went contrary to all Gentile cultures. To the Ephesians Paul wrote, "But fornication and impurity of any kind, or greed, must not even be mentioned among you, as is proper among saints. Entirely out of place is obscene, silly, and vulgar talk, but instead, let there be thanksgiving. Be sure of this, that no fornicator or impure person, or one who is greedy (that is, an idolater), has any inheritance in the kingdom of Christ and of God."[1] Paul's advice, following Jesus, is to bless one's enemies and to forgive one another.

Paul was chosen by Christ to take the Gospel to Israel and the Gentile nations— to reveal *God's plan* of salvation. It was a plan of salvation for every human heart not just for a particular nation or race. Carrying out this commission inevitably made Paul (after Jesus) the greatest culture warrior of all time. But Paul's challenge was *not just an ancient society—but our very own*. Today, his words and theology wage a relentless fight against those who propose *another gospel* revised by mankind to fit the standards and customs of our society. Pauline thought still challenges our tendency *to worship the creature instead of*

---

[1] Eph. 5:3-5 NRSV.

the Creator. Paul's exhortations call us out on questions of sexual immorality, greed, dishonesty, hesitancy to forgive, and self gratification. His matchless concepts about Christian love overpower our puny efforts to express this most essential human emotion. Paul calls us to a *world view* where Christ is God's supreme answer to our constant woes, worries, sins, and inability to save ourselves and our society.

Paul is still evangelizing. His message speaks clearly to our culture. His immortal letters continue to turn people around—bringing them to faith in Jesus Christ—to forgiveness, peace, love and joy—to the fulfillment of eternal life by the power of the Holy Spirit.

Addendum

Some of the other great passages in Paul's letters

"But when the fullness of time had come, God sent his Son, born of a woman, born under the law, in order to redeem those who were under the law, so that we might receive adoption as children." Galatians 4:4,5 NRSV.

"We know that all things work together for good for those who love God, who are called according to his purpose." Romans 8:28 NRSV.

"For I am not ashamed of the gospel; it is the power of God

for salvation to everyone who has faith, to the Jew first and also to the Greek." Romans !:16 NRSV.

"God is faithful, and he will not let you be tempted beyond your strength, but with the temptation will also provide the way of escape, that you may be able to endure it." 1Corinthians 10:13b RSV.

"He (God) has delivered us from the dominion of darkness and transferred us to the kingdom of his beloved Son, in whom we have redemption, the forgiveness of sins."
Colossians 1:13, 14 RSV (my parenthesis).

"For the love of money is a root of all kinds of evil, and in their eagerness to be rich, some have wandered away from the faith and pierced themselves with many pains."
1 Timothy 6:10 NRSV.

"Besides this you know what hour it is, how it is full time now for you to wake from sleep. For salvation is nearer to us now than when we first believed; the night is far gone, the day is at hand. Let us then cast off the works of darkness and put on the armor of light…" Romans 13:11,12. RSV.

Paul's witnessing speech to the synagogue at Pisidian Antioch—Acts 13:16b-42 RSV

"Men of Israel and you that fear God, listen. The God of this people Israel chose our fathers and made the people great during their stay in the land of Egypt, and with uplifted arm he led them out of it. And for about forty years he bore with them in the wilderness. And when he had destroyed seven nations in the land of Canaan, he gave them their land as an inheritance, for about four hundred and fifty years. And after that he gave them judges until Samuel the prophet. Then they asked for a king, and God gave them Saul the son of Kish, a man of the tribe of Benjamin, for forty years. And when he had removed him, he raised up David to be their king; of whom he testified and said, 'I have found in David the son of Jesse a man after my heart, who will do all my will.' Of this man's posterity God has brought to Israel a Savior, Jesus, as he promised. Before his coming John had preached a baptism of repentance to all the people of Israel. And as John was finishing his course, he said, 'What do you suppose that I am? I am not he. No, but after me one is coming, the sandals of whose feet I am not worthy to untie.'

"Brethren, sons of the family of Abraham, and those among you that fear God, to us has been sent the message of this salvation. For those who live in Jerusalem and their rulers, because they did not recognize him nor understand the utterances of the prophets, which are read every Sabbath, fulfilled these by condemning him. Though they could charge him with nothing deserving death, yet they asked Pilate to have him killed. And when they had fulfilled all that was written of him, they took him down from the tree, and laid him in a tomb. But God raised him from the dead; and for many days he appeared to those who came up with him from Galilee to Jerusalem, who are now his witnesses to the people. And we bring you the good news that what God promised to the fathers, this he has fulfilled to us their children by raising Jesus; as also it is written in the second psalm:

'Thou art my Son, today I have begotten thee.'
And as for the fact that he raised him from the
dead, no more to return to corruption, he spoke in
this way, 'I will give you the holy and sure
blessing of David.' Therefore he says also in
another psalm, 'Thou wilt not let thy Holy One
see corruption.' For David, after he had served
the counsel of God in his own generation, fell
asleep, and was laid with his fathers, and saw
corruption; but he whom God raised up saw no
corruption.

"Let it be known to you therefore, brethren, that through this man forgiveness of sins is proclaimed to you, and by him every one that believes is freed from everything from which you could not be freed by the law of Moses.

"Beware, therefore, lest there come upon you what is said in the prophets:

'Behold, you scoffers, and wonder, and perish; for I do a deed in your days, a deed you will never believe, if one declares it to you.' "

As they went out, the people begged that these things might be told them the next Sabbath.

Bibliography

Dunn, James D.G. 1998. *The Theology of Paul the Apostle.* Grand Rapids, Michigan.

Schnelle, Udo. 2005. *Apostle Paul.* English Translation. Grand Rapids, Michigan.

Bruce, F.F. 2000. *Paul: Apostle of the Heart Set Free.* In U.S.A. Grand Rapids, Michigan.

Swindoll, Charles R. 2002. *Paul, A Man of Grace and Grit.* Nashville, Tennessee.

Butler, John G. 1995. *Paul, The Missionary Apostle.* Clinton, Iowa.

Wangerin, Walter Jr. 2000. *Paul.* Grand Rapids, Michigan.

Barclay, William. 1958. *The Mind of St. Paul.* New York, New York.

Stott, John R.W. 1990. *The Message of Acts.* In U.S.A. Madison, Wisconsin.
Stott, John R.W. 1968. *The Message of Galatians.* In U.S.A. Madison, Wisconsin.

Lucas, R.C. 1980 *The Message of Colossians and Philemon.* In U.S.A. Madison, Wisconsin.

Stott, John R.W. 1994. *The Message of Romans.* In U.S.A. Downers Grove, Illinois.

Prior, David 1985 *The Message of 1 Corinthians.* In U.S.A. Downers Grove, Illinois

Butler, Trent C. Ph.D. 1991. *Holman Bible Dictionary.* Nashville, Tennessee.

Miller, Madeleine S.& Miller, J.Lane. 1952, '54, '55, '56,'58,'59,'61. *Harper's Bible Dictionary.* New York, New York.

Gills, James P., M.D.& Woodward, Tom Ph.D. 2002. *Darwinism under the Microscope.* .Lake Mary, Florida.

Metzger, Dr. Bruce M. 1991. *NRSV Exhaustive Concordance.* Nashville, Tennessee.

Strong, James LL.S., S.T.D.   1990. *Strong's Exhaustive Concordance of the Bible.* Nashville, Tennessee

The Holy Bible, Revised Standard Version (cited RSV). 1946, 1952. Toronto, New York, Edinburgh.

The Holy Bible, New Revised Standard Version (cited NRSV). 1989. New York, New York.

Life Application Study Bible, New American Standard Bible (cited NASB). Updated edition. 2000. Grand Rapids, Michigan.

The Holy Bible, King James Version (cited KJV).

The Holy Bible, New International Version (cited NIV). 1978. Grand Rapids, Michigan.